Emily grabbed for the phone and qui
before it was even up to her ear. "Dor
packedwiththecarloadedandeverything
aged to say without taking a breath. Ther
no response on the other end, she asked more slowly, "Holly.
Are you there?" When a loud sniffle was her response, Emily's
heart sank.

"Holly, what is it?"

"I'm not coming to PCU tomorrow, Em."

"What do you mean? You're coming up on Sunday instead?"

"No, I mean I'm not coming to PCU this year at all. I got a
letter the other day saying that my grant fell through. My parents have been trying to find some way to make up the difference, but it's just not going to happen. The money isn't there. It
looks like I'll have to go to junior college here this year and
reapply for financial aid in the spring."

"But we've been planning to go to PCU together since
sophomore year!"

◆

Will Emily survive college life without her best friend?
Find out in Freshman Blues, *first in the exciting new PCU series!*

NUMBER **1**

FRESHMAN BLUES

BY WENDY LEE NENTWIG

This is a work of fiction. The characters, incidents, and dialogues are products of the author's imagination and are not to be construed as real. Any resemblance to actual events or persons, living or dead, is entirely coincidental.

FRESHMAN BLUES
published by Palisades
a part of the Questar publishing family

© 1996 by Wendy Lee Nentwig
International Standard Book Number: 0-88070-947-2

Cover photography by Mike Houska
Cover designed by Kevin Keller
Printed in the United States of America

For my mother,

Lin Doyle,

*who insisted on ironing every piece of clothing I owned
before dropping me off at college and
continued to be supportive
long after my cap and gown
were packed away.*

ACKNOWLEDGMENTS

To my sisters, Tamera Levin and Barbara Holmstrom, who keep me coming home. To my nephews, Garrett, Corbett and Kyle for sharing your baseball games, crafts and trips to Disneyland with me. To Dad, Bonnie and Mike because I don't say thanks enough. To Robin Jones Gunn, my identical cousin, thanks bunches. To Roberta Green Ahmanson for trying to make me a journalist. To Leslie Morris who knows what it's like to be locked in a room with a computer for months on end, thanks for the French help and the memories of Graan voor Visch. To all those who had the dubious honor of rooming with me in Horton Hall during my Biola years, thanks for making it more fun than I thought it could ever be and giving me countless story ideas. And finally, to Lisa Hausdorfer, college roommate and much, much more, thanks for understanding it all.

1

Emily Stewart struggled to her feet, balancing unsteadily on legs cramped from sitting too long in the same position. As she stretched her arms over her head of long brown curls and surveyed the mess she had made of her bedroom she wondered how she would ever be ready to leave for college in just twelve hours. It was ironic since she had been getting ready for her freshman year at Pacific Cascades University for the past three months—actually, the past three years.

When her dad had taken a job as senior pastor of a small church in Central Oregon three years earlier, the Stewart family had to leave their long-time home near Portland. At the time, Emily and her best friend Holly were devastated at the prospect of being separated. In the weeks before the move, they consoled themselves by making a pact to room together at college. Since then, they had written letters every week, filled with dreams of what college would be like.

Over the past few months the girls had been consumed with collecting things to decorate their dorm-room-to-be. Emily had accumulated a new alarm clock, several black and white Ansel Adams prints, a thick green rug, and new towels that matched the green and blue plaid quilts she and Holly had purchased over spring break. Emily even had a new fuzzy green bathrobe since she and Holly would be sharing a bathroom with two other girls in their suite. The biggest item, though, was the mini-refrigerator they had started saving for immediately after receiving their acceptance notices from PCU. By August, the pile in the corner of Emily's room, which she had started referring to as "my new life," had actually become a huge mound that seemingly threatened to take over the whole house. She just hoped she could get it all packed in time.

As Emily stretched to get the blood flowing back into her cramped limbs, her 15-year-old sister, Kate, burst in clutching a rumpled gray Oregon State sweatshirt to her chest.

"Okay, so I did have your ugly old sweatshirt after all. But I still take no responsibility for losing your sandals," she blurted out. Only as she paused for breath did she fully take in Emily's uncharacteristically trashed room, adding loudly, "You are *so* dead when mom sees this. It looks like something exploded in here!"

Emily grabbed the sweatshirt, which she was sure had spent several weeks rolled up in a ball in Kate's mess of a closet, and put it with her other college-bound stuff. She felt it was important to have something to show her loyalty to her home state. Besides, this sweatshirt was worn to just the right softness and was a favorite companion on her morning jogs. The sandals she chose to overlook, even though she knew her sister had worn them last and Kate was notorious for losing things. After all, hadn't she just last night at dinner insisted she had nothing to do with the sweatshirt's disappearance and now here it was?

The sandals will probably surface around Christmas or with the first snowfall, Emily thought. Oh, well. As an almost-college-freshman Emily felt she was too mature to fight with her younger sister anymore. At least over something like sandals.

Uninvited, Kate plopped down on the only corner of the bed not covered with Emily's belongings and began pawing through the items nearest her.

"Isn't there something you'd rather be doing?" Emily suggested.

"Nope. Just thought I'd spend a little time with my favorite sister before she leaves for college," Kate replied, smiling much too sweetly.

"I'm your *only* sister," Emily pointed out dryly, wondering what Kate really wanted. Luckily it didn't take long to find out.

"I thought you might not be able to fit all your clothes in those tiny little suitcases. I just wanted to let you know that if you need to leave anything behind, I'd be happy to look after it for you. Like your purple sweater for example."

Before Emily had a chance to tell her sister there was no way she would get within ten feet of that sweater, their older brother, Ryan, poked his head in the door, surveyed the situation, and began to offer his unsolicited advice.

"Hey what's with all the mess? I told you, packing for college is no big deal. It's just like an extended camping trip. Throw a few changes of clothes and a blanket or two into a duffel bag, and you're ready to go."

"That may have worked for you, brother dear," Emily began, a bit condescendingly, "but remember, I visited you at college last year and saw that depressing cell you called a dorm room. I have no intention of following in your footsteps. In fact, I hope no one who saw that room holds your lack of taste against me!"

"Oh, I'm wounded," Ryan shot back. He clutched his chest, as if Emily's words had physically injured him, before breaking into a smile.

Emily tried to ignore his theatrics, but Ryan wouldn't let it go.

"Just remember, I'm leaving for PCU at 8:00 A.M. sharp, with or without you," he threatened in his annoying big brother tone.

Emily gave him an exasperated look and turned her attention back to the job at hand. "I'm sure I would get a lot more done if I didn't have so many interruptions," she said pointedly, hoping he and Kate would both take her hint. Amazingly, it worked.

Emily managed to pack another bag before the next interruption. After nearly twenty minutes had passed, her dad appeared in the doorway holding the cordless phone out to her. She was so wrapped up in what she was doing she hadn't even heard it ring.

"It's Holly," he said as he passed her the receiver.

Emily grabbed for the phone and quickly began talking before it was even up to her ear. "Don'teventellmeyou'reall-packedwiththecarloaded-andeverythingorI'lldie!" she managed to say without taking a breath. Then, realizing there was no response on the other end, she asked more slowly, "Holly? Are you there?" When a loud sniffle was her response, Emily's heart sank.

"Holly, what is it?"

"I'm not coming to PCU tomorrow, Em."

"What do you mean? You're coming up on Sunday instead?"

"No, I mean I'm not coming to PCU this year at all. I got a letter the other day saying that my grant fell through. My parents have been trying to find some way to make up the difference, but it's just not going to happen. The money isn't there. It looks like I'll have to go to junior college here this year and reapply for financial aid in the spring."

"But we've been planning to go to PCU together since sophomore year!" Emily reminded her friend, fully aware that Holly knew this, but at a loss for anything else to say.

"I know," Holly squeaked, then sniffed again.

As the shock began to wear off, questions flooded Emily's mind. Immediately she blurted out, "Who am I going to room with?"

"I bet it will be someone really nice and I'll be stuck here sharing a bathroom with my little brothers. I can't believe this is happening!" Kate wailed.

Her friend's words gave Emily's conscience a jolt. "I'm really sorry. You find out you don't get to go away to college, and all I can do is worry about myself. I know how bummed you must be."

"Bummed is an understatement," agreed Holly sadly.

"Holly, I know it's not the same but I'll write every week. And I promise not to have a bit of fun until you finally come and we're roommates as planned," Emily vowed.

"I appreciate that, but I know you're going to have a great time." Holly struggled to sound positive, but her disappointment came through in her voice.

"You can still come visit at least," Emily consoled.

"Thanks for the invite. You know I'll take you up on it. But now I'd better let you go. You probably still have packing to do."

Emily started to protest, but then realized how anxious she was to get off the phone and collect her thoughts. She said a subdued good-bye and turned off the phone.

As she curled up on her bed Emily struggled to figure out why God would allow this to happen. They had been planning for so long, and now everything was ruined! She tried to think happy thoughts, but even the image of herself surrounded by tons of new friends at college wasn't enough to stop the tears of disappointment from spilling down her cheeks.

2

Emily shifted uncomfortably in the passenger seat of her brother's beat-up, gray pickup as it flew down the highway. They had been on the road for more than two hours but weren't even halfway to Seattle yet. Still, Emily was grateful for the opportunity to nap after a restless, tearful night and an emotional good-bye that morning. Just yesterday, she had been so excited to start college. But now all she felt was apprehension. All her mental pictures of the perfect college life included Holly. Without her best friend joining her, Emily began to wonder if maybe she shouldn't have just stayed home, too. Their college dream had fallen apart, and much of Emily's confidence had crumbled with it. As a result, it had been really difficult to leave home, watching her family get smaller and smaller through the truck's grimy rear window.

Their mother had wanted to make the trip with them to help her daughter settle in at college, but Emily had dissuaded her when they discussed it earlier that week. It was such a long drive and both parents had attended orientation weekend at PCU with Ryan last year, Emily had argued. Besides, her dad had just begun a new Sunday morning series and his preaching was always better when Mrs. Stewart was sitting in the front row. And Emily hadn't wanted to look like a baby needing her mom to help her move in. She was sure she could manage on her own, Emily assured them. But now she wasn't so certain.

"Isn't it about time for a lunch break?" Emily groaned to her brother.

"I wasn't planning to stop for half an hour," Ryan answered. "That's the halfway point. You should have grabbed something when we stopped for gas, like I told you to."

Emily sighed. Since Ryan was driving, he insisted that he was also in control of all stops. This included when, where, and for how long. The only area of their trip Emily could exercise any control over was music. It was a long-standing Stewart rule that the front seat passenger had control of the stereo. Eager for a diversion, Emily reached down and scooped Ryan's tape case off the floor. She tried not to think about food as she popped in a cassette, but just then a Burger King whizzed by her window. Her stomach rumbled as if on cue. It was going to be a very long day.

"Here, have a piece of gum," Ryan said, holding out a stick of the black licorice gum he always chewed.

"Gross," Emily responded, turning up her nose at the offer. "That stuff makes your tongue all black and is totally disgusting. Why can't you just buy some Trident or something like a normal person?"

Ryan shrugged and slid the gum back into his shirt pocket.

It was actually more like an hour before they pulled up in front of a rather decrepit-looking fast food place. A neon sign out front flashed "Burgers, Fries, Shakes," and it didn't even seem to have a name, but Emily had her door open before the truck had made a complete stop. As she bit into a warm, juicy burger a few minutes later, she made a mental note to let her brother choose the next tape when they got back on the road.

With a few hours sleep to her credit and a full stomach, Emily felt a little more optimistic as they resumed their journey.

"Okay, I'm starting to get excited about college now," Emily said, turning to her brother. "So why don't you tell me what I can expect. I mean, you're going to be an orientation leader this week, after all."

It seemed like a reasonable request, but apparently it wasn't. Instead of telling Emily about all the great activities she could be a part of and assuring her she would finally have a busy social life, Ryan became the voice of doom.

"The most important thing is to get involved in a local church right away, Emmie. And of course you'll want to steer clear of the frat parties. The only reason anyone goes is to get drunk. Also, you really have to watch getting behind on the reading for your lecture courses. Midterms creep up on you pretty fast."

Emily felt like her parents were there after all. She knew her brother meant well, but it annoyed her that he didn't trust her to be smart enough to figure these things out for herself. Besides, all his advice was just making her more nervous.

"Thanks, Dad," she said, rolling her eyes at her brother.

Her sarcasm seemed lost on him, though, as Ryan droned on with his list of don'ts. Emily tried to remain calm, but when he all but forbade her to join a sorority because he didn't want her dating any frat guys, that was the last straw.

"Look, Ryan, I think we better get a few things straight right now," Emily began, struggling to control her temper. "In case you haven't noticed, I'm not twelve anymore. And contrary to popular belief, I can take care of myself. I don't need you telling me what clubs I can join and who I can and can't date. I am perfectly capable of making my own decisions, even if I'm not great at everything like you are!"

"Whoa, what are you talking about?" Ryan looked and sounded stunned.

Emily hadn't meant to let that last part slip out, although it was something she had struggled with all through high school. Now she felt she was forced to explain.

"I'm talking about spending the last four years of my life trying to escape from your shadow—captain of the varsity basketball team, all-league in baseball, senior class president. There wasn't anything I could do that you hadn't already done better and a year earlier. Even last year when you went away to college your reputation stayed behind, haunting the halls of Madison High . . . and me. You even ruined my social life! All your guy friends treat me like I'm *their* little sister, too. And the boys my age are so in awe of you, they're afraid to come near me because they know how overprotective you are."

Ryan stared at his sister in amazement. "I had no idea you felt this way. Why haven't you ever said anything?"

Emily was genuinely surprised. How could Ryan not know about the negative effect he'd had on her social life in high school? She'd always assumed he knew and just didn't care.

"I guess I felt like nothing was going to change while I was still at home. But I hoped college would be different—that I might finally be known for something other than being Ryan Stewart's little sister," Emily explained, shrugging self-consciously. She really hadn't meant to get into all of this with Ryan today, but she figured she might as well finish what she started.

"Look, I agreed to go to the same university because of the tuition break Mom and Dad will get having two of us there. But this is not going to be like high school where we knew all the same people and ran into each other every Friday night at the movie theater. With 1,500 students on campus, I think we can coexist quite happily at PCU without seeing much of each other at all if you go your way and let me go mine."

"I was only trying to look out for you, you know," Ryan said defensively.

Emily sighed. "I know, and I'm sure Mom and Dad asked you to keep an eye on me at college. But I don't need your protection. Am I making myself clear?"

Emily knew her brother had a tendency to get a little carried away with his good intentions, and it was time she put her foot down. She remembered all too well the time she found out he had told all his basketball teammates that his little sister was off limits to any of them. And she suspected there had been similar declarations made to any other guy who had shown the least bit of interest in her during high school. Well, she was through spending every Saturday night with the girls!

"Is that all, Emmie?" Ryan asked, an edge to his voice.

"Actually, now that you mention it there is one more thing. Could you please not call me Emmie? It makes me sound like such a baby."

Ryan nodded his head but didn't meet his sister's eye. She knew he was upset, but she also knew she needed to say what she did. With that taken care of, Emily turned up the volume on the stereo a few notches, settled back on the vinyl seat and closed her eyes, trying to forget the stressful confrontation with

19

her brother by letting the music wash over her.

The silence was broken only when Seattle's skyline finally came into view later that afternoon.

"Look, it's the Space Needle!" Emily exclaimed, pointing toward the 600-foot-high structure which looked like something that belonged at Disneyland. Ryan didn't seem very interested, but Emily's heart was racing. She willed herself to remain calm as they reached the city limits. But despite her best efforts, all her anxieties about college bubbled to the surface, making her feel like a bottle of Coke that had been shaken.

Am I really ready for college? Emily wondered. Before she could answer herself she saw the sign that read: "Welcome to Pacific Cascades University."

It looked like she would find out soon enough.

3

Ryan wisely chose to wait in the truck while Emily went to get her room key. As she stood in a long line that wound all the way outdoors, she stared up at McNeil Hall, the brick building that would be her home for the next nine months. A good part of the dorm wall was covered by a brightly painted sign that read: "Set Sail for Knowledge at PCU," and a huge cardboard anchor hung suspended from a second story window. *Looks like the administration decided on a nautical theme for registration,* Emily concluded. *How cheesy. Now this is the kind of thing Ryan should have warned me about.*

Just then, a too-cheerful student dressed like Popeye greeted her with a loud "Ahoy, there!" After pulling Emily's card out of a file she handed over a set of keys, a list of rules for living in the dorms, and a schedule of orientation activities. Emily was then herded into another line where another sailor-suit-clad student, this one with a colorful parrot perched on his shoulder, snapped her picture. A few minutes later "Parrot Boy" handed Emily her student ID card, which he explained she would need to get into the cafeteria, as well as her dorm after hours. "So you'd better not lose it," he warned.

Feeling overwhelmed, Emily made her way back to the truck and grabbed the two suitcases nearest the tailgate.

"I'm not interfering in your life if I help you carry your things upstairs, am I?" Ryan asked jokingly.

"Actually I'd appreciate the help, but no complaining about how much stuff I brought," Emily warned.

Emily staggered a little as she pushed open the door to her suite while still juggling her suitcases. Once inside, she barely had time to scan the sparsely furnished living room before Ryan herded her toward the bedroom on the left, marked 216A. As they crossed the threshold, Emily heard Ryan suck in his breath.

"And I thought *you* brought a lot of stuff!" he exclaimed.

They set Emily's things on her bare mattress and stared across the room. Obviously her roommate had already made an appearance, although she was nowhere to be found at present. Clothes, shoes, CDs, and books were strewn all over. The bed wasn't made yet, but a stack of bedding was balanced on a portable TV, and a laptop computer was perched on the desk, precariously close to the edge. Emily was amazed at the sheer volume of things this mystery roommate had fit into her small half of the room. Her excess made Emily's side of the room look even more empty.

"C'mon, let's go get another load out of the truck," Emily said, pulling on Ryan's sleeve. He was still standing there with his mouth open. She was glad her new roommate wasn't around to see their reactions.

After several more trips up and down the stairs, they finished unloading her things. Ryan stood around uncomfortably for a few minutes, then, wiping his grimy hands on his jeans, he left to settle into his own place across campus in Mercer Hall.

"Thanks for your help," Emily called out after him. *At least we aren't in the same dorm,* she thought, as she closed the door and whispered a silent prayer of thanks.

Finally, Emily was alone and able to fully explore her new home. Her suite was halfway down the dorm's carpeted hallway, on the left hand side. The front door opened directly into a small living room with an ugly couch, some particle board bookshelves, and a big, overstuffed chair that was leaking its foam filling onto the green shag carpet. There were bedroom doors at the far end of the living room, one on either side, and a dark little bathroom off to the left of the suite's front door.

Emily wondered if the other suite-mates had arrived yet. Just as she returned to her bedroom, the door to 216A flew open.

"Oh, I didn't know anyone else was here," a girl said to Emily, more as a statement than an apology, then added, "You're not Susanna, are you?"

"Uh, no. I'm Emily. Emily Stewart," Emily managed to get out.

"Yeah, they told me when I registered that my roommate wasn't going to show. I had been assigned someone named Susanna. We'd even written a few times over the summer to get to know each other, but for some reason or other she's not coming."

"My roommate couldn't come at the last minute either," Emily offered, eager to find any bit of common ground with this still nameless girl.

"I guess we'll be roommates then."

"Well, nice to meet you…uh…?" Emily stammered. When her new roommate didn't fill in the blank Emily finally blurted out, "Do you have a name?"

"Of course I do," the roommate answered in a tone that seemed to imply it was a stupid question. "I'm Cooper…Ellis."

"Nice to meet you, Cooper," Emily said, but the girl had already turned away and was cramming piles of clothes into the dresser near her bed.

Emily tried not to stare, but it was hard. *Even Mom, who has better manners than anyone I've ever met, would have a hard time not staring at this girl,* Emily thought. She gazed across the room again, taking in the tall, thin brunette who moved through the mess around her like a ballerina. She was wearing a pair of black velvet jeans and a shiny silver blouse with the bottom two buttons undone, barely showing her stomach. On her feet were strappy black sandals, and on each hand were several big silver rings, all slightly different from each other. She even wore one on her thumb.

Her dark hair was sleek and shiny, falling just below her shoulders, and she had olive-toned skin that most girls only dreamed about. Emily tried to turn away, but as Cooper reached for another pile of shirts, Emily couldn't help noticing one last thing—her perfectly manicured fingernails were painted the color of dried blood. What was even more amazing was that on her, it looked good.

Emily glanced down at her own clothes and pulled absently at the frayed edge of her denim shorts. They were her favorite pair and had taken forever to break in and get faded to just the right shade of light blue. Today, she had topped them with an old red and blue striped rugby shirt of Ryan's. To finish the ensemble she had pulled on her favorite hiking boots over red socks and pulled her hair back in a loose ponytail with a few curls escaping around her face.

This morning the outfit had seemed like the perfect choice for moving into the dorm, but maybe she had been wrong. She struggled to remember what the other students in line at the registration table had been wearing. She couldn't recall anything specific, but since she hadn't felt out of place, she concluded that most of them must have been dressed similarly.

"Pretty ugly room, huh?" Emily ventured. The bedroom was rather boring—twin beds with metal frames and old stained mattresses, identical small wooden dressers, and utilitarian desks. The green shag carpeting didn't extend into the bedrooms. Instead, grayish square tiles covered the floor, except for a spot under Emily's desk where one tile was missing.

Cooper mumbled in agreement.

Just as Emily was working up the courage to take another stab at conversation and ask Cooper if either of their suitemates had arrived, she heard a door slam and voices fill the living room. Poking her head out of her bedroom, Emily saw a man in jeans and expensive-looking cowboy boots setting several pieces of matching luggage on the ugly avocado-green couch. Behind him was a girl with thick, shoulder-length brown hair, dressed in neatly pressed khaki shorts and a white polo shirt. There was also an attractive woman in linen shorts and a casual blouse. Upon spotting Emily, the girl crossed the room and extended her hand.

"Hi, I'm Kenzie and these are my parents, John and Peggy Dawson," she said with a slight twang and a smile that showed off deep dimples.

Emily gratefully shook hands and introduced herself. Then, making a face in the direction of the sofa, she commented, "Wow! When they said our rooms would be furnished, I thought that would be a good thing!"

"Looks like it needs to be fumigated!" Kenzie agreed. "But my dad'll probably fall asleep on it anyway. We've had a long trip."

"Where'd you come from?" Emily asked.

"Nashville, although we drove out, making a side-trip to Wyoming to see my uncle."

Emily was impressed. She'd never left the West Coast.

"Oh, I only came up from Oregon. But I can tell you, one day bouncing around in my brother's truck was enough. I'm convinced that thing has absolutely no shocks!"

"Your brother has a truck? I love trucks!" Kenzie exclaimed. "But a long trip with no shocks could be a bummer. And speaking of bummers," she glanced over one shoulder at her parents, "We need to get the rest of my stuff out of the car. It was nice to meet you, Emily."

Emily considered offering to help, but didn't want to be too pushy. Instead she reluctantly said good-bye and went back to her bedroom and her own unpacking.

Cooper had been busy setting up her stereo on shiny black shelves she must have brought from home and now was digging through the mess on her bed in search of something. At last, she triumphantly held up a CD and headed over to the stereo.

"The perfect 'moving into the dorm' music," she announced.

As the first song filled the room, Emily tried not to let her opinion of Cooper's choice show, but it was difficult. Emily knew it was too much to hope they might have the same taste in music, but this was worse than she imagined. She didn't recognize the band, but she knew she didn't like it. True, Emily was used to listening only to Christian music—it was all her parents allowed the kids to listen to at home—but it was not like she expected it to be the music of choice for most of the students at PCU. Still, this was just loud and obnoxious. Emily couldn't help thinking wistfully that if Holly were there, they would have no trouble agreeing on a soundtrack for their first day of college. *Well, at least Kenzie seems nice.*

Trying her best to tune out Cooper's music, she stretched out on her bed to read over the schedule she'd been handed during check-in. She found out that orientation groups didn't meet until the next day, giving students a chance to settle in and spend a few last hours with their families. But there would be a big barbecue on the main quad in an hour or so. It was a good thing, because she was getting hungry again. Emily spent the time before dinner getting her half of the room organized. She set up her portable stereo and wished she could put in a tape, but Cooper's music still dominated the room. Emily tried several times to start a conversation with her roommate, but got only short answers.

"So where are you from?" Emily asked during a break between songs.

"New York City," Cooper answered as the next song started.

New York City? Emily always thought that only actors, models, and Donald Trump lived there. She hadn't realized normal people actually called it home. But then again, Cooper hardly seemed normal.

As the time for the barbecue drew near, Emily brushed out

her curly hair, pulled it back with a headband, and added a little blush and light lipstick to her tan face. Her blue eyes could have used a little something to bring them out, but her mascara had disappeared somewhere in the clutter. Before heading out the door she grabbed a sweatshirt and tied it around her waist. She knew how cool the Pacific Northwest nights could be. As she tucked her keys and the all-important ID card in her shorts pocket, she wondered if she should invite Cooper to walk over with her. Not in the mood to be shot down again by her antisocial roommate, she quickly decided against it. Maybe she would run into Kenzie on the way.

As Emily neared the quad, a wave of loneliness swept over her. Everyone seemed to be with their families, and as she stood in line waiting for a hot dog, she couldn't help feeling a little sorry for herself. It didn't affect her appetite, though. When her turn came she heaped her plate with not just a hot dog, but with chips, potato salad, and several cookies before reaching into a large ice-filled garbage can and pulling out a can of Coke.

With her hands full, Emily began to look around for a place to sit. She didn't see Kenzie or anyone she recognized, but that wasn't surprising since she really didn't know anyone. At last she spotted Ryan sitting under a tree with a group of students who looked too relaxed to be freshmen. They were probably other orientation leaders. After her long speech in the truck about needing her space, Emily couldn't bring herself to join her brother. She finally sat down on the edge of a fountain situated in the middle of the quad. At least she would have something to look at while she ate her solitary dinner, and the sound of the flowing water was soothing.

Just as Emily popped the last bite of hot dog into her mouth, she noticed Cooper sitting with a couple who were too old to be students and too young to be her parents. They didn't look anything like Cooper, either, since they blended in easily. Whoever they were, Cooper seemed to have no trouble talking to them, Emily noticed, as her roommate threw back her head and laughed.

As Emily made her way back to her dorm room she couldn't help thinking that if this was college, Holly sure wasn't missing much.

4

mily was glad she hadn't finished all of her unpacking before the barbecue, as it gave her something to do during the long hours that now stretched before her. When she entered her empty room, she popped in an old Margaret Becker tape and began to sing along softly as she worked.

Emily had always loved to sing and was often told she had a beautiful voice, but she wasn't comfortable performing in public. She had joined her high school chorale mainly because they were one of the most fun groups on campus and the promise of a spring trip to Disneyland was just the incentive Emily needed to work at overcoming her stage fright. Since then, she had been persuaded to sing a few solos in church, but being on stage was still uncomfortable for her. Still, she thought she might try out for one of PCU's smaller singing groups as a way to make friends. Besides, her parents had urged her to "not let the talent God gave you go to waste." She decided she'd have to see how intimidated she felt when tryouts rolled around.

Cooper had done a little more decorating, Emily noticed. There was a real working stoplight perched on her roommate's bookshelf, and a metal sign that read BOMB SHELTER hung above her bed. Cooper had stuck bright red footprints, the kind used in dancing classes to help teach the foxtrot or the mambo. Emily couldn't help noticing that nothing matched, in contrast to her own color-coordinated things. She tried not to think about it as she made her bed with her crisp new sheets.

As the night wore on, Cooper still did not return from the barbecue. In fact, the entire dorm seemed deserted. In the movies, dorms were always loud, with people constantly coming and going, hanging out windows, or congregating in the halls. But McNeil Hall was eerily quiet. With no distractions, however, Emily was able to unpack all of her stuff, store her empty duffel bags and backpack neatly under the bed, and even lug the mini-refrigerator out into a corner of the living room. She hoped her suite-mates wouldn't mind her taking up the space, but it seemed all right since they would probably use it, too. She even christened it by filling it with a few Cherry Cokes from the vending machine she found at the end of the hall.

With everything in its place, Emily sat down at her new desk, pulled out a few sheets of the stationery her youth pastor's wife had given her as a going-away-to-college present, and wrote a depressing letter to Holly. At least she didn't have to downplay all the fun she was having in an attempt to spare her friend's feelings. After recounting all the horrible events of the day in great detail, Emily placed a stamp on the thin envelope and set it on the edge of her desk so she would remember to mail it in the morning. Then, with nothing else to do, Emily decided she might as well get ready for bed.

Just as she got under the covers, the door opened and Cooper stepped inside.

"Hi," she said absently, tossing a black leather jacket on her rumpled bed. "Did you end up going to that ice cream thingie?"

She was so startled that Cooper was actually talking to her, it took Emily a few seconds to realize she had no idea what her roommate was talking about. As a result, "Excuse me?" was the only response she could manage.

"You got your voice-mail message didn't you?"

"Voice-mail message?" Emily repeated, feeling like the bird belonging to "Parrot Boy" from registration.

Cooper rolled her eyes and explained that their R.A. had called just after Emily left, inviting them to an ice-cream social/get-to-know-your-dorm-mates bash in the third floor lounge.

"Since orientation groups don't meet until tomorrow, they thought some of the incoming freshmen might not have anything to do tonight. You weren't here, so she left you a message in your voice-mail box," Cooper concluded, as if receiving voice-mail messages was the most natural thing in the world.

"I...I didn't even know I had a voice-mail box," Emily stammered, hating the way her new roommate was able to make her feel so flustered. "And what's an R.A.?"

"Resident Assistant," Cooper explained, sounding exasperated. "The voice mail is hooked up to the phones. There was a whole sheet explaining how to use it in the packet they gave you when you registered. I just assumed you read it. I already recorded my message this afternoon. It was really easy. I would have written you a note, but my aunt and her fiancé were waiting for me over at the barbecue and I was already late."

Emily knew it wasn't really Cooper's fault, but she also knew that if she had taken the call, she would have left a note. It was a fitting ending to an already disastrous day. Emily could only hope that the next day would be better. It would be Sunday, and Emily was planning to walk to a church she had noticed as she and Ryan drove in that afternoon. The old white building looked kind of homey and inviting, and it was only a few blocks from campus. There was even a sign out front that told when services began, so she didn't have to search through the phone book or call. *I'm sure I'll feel better after going to church,* Emily thought as she drifted off to sleep. *I certainly couldn't feel any worse.*

The sun was already shining brightly when Emily's alarm pierced the quiet. She woke immediately since she wasn't used to the sound the new clock made. It was definitely louder than the one she had left at home. *I won't be oversleeping and missing class, that's for sure,* Emily thought. She glanced over to see if the noise had disturbed Cooper, but her roommate, buried deep under a thick down comforter, hadn't moved.

Emily quietly made her way to the shower and then got ready as silently as possible. She opened the blinds on her window, but that didn't provide much light as it was a typical gray Seattle day. Still, it seemed kind of rude to turn on her lamp, since Cooper was asleep. As she rummaged in her top drawer —feeling around blindly for her hairbrush—Emily couldn't help thinking once again that if Holly were there, this wouldn't be an issue. They'd be getting ready for church together with the lights on. Also, Emily would have someone to sit with during the service. They would probably stop for doughnuts on the way home, lingering for hours over hot chocolate as they talked about everything and nothing.

Emily couldn't quite envision the same scenario happening with Cooper. She doubted seriously that her odd roommate had ever even set foot inside a church before. Emily chalked it up to just one more thing she and Cooper didn't have in common as she ran her fingers through her damp curls, grabbed her Bible, and closed the door softly behind her.

The walk was calming for Emily, who loved being outdoors, but as soon as she reached Pacific Christian Church her stomach lurched. It was so weird to feel out of place at church. She had always been the pastor's daughter, the one who walked the other new kids to Sunday School and knew where all the nursery supplies were kept. This was a whole new sensation. What if they made her stand up and introduce herself? Emily peered into the sanctuary that was about half full and quickly slid into an empty pew near the back. She studied a hymnal and tried to look inconspicuous, but she felt like there was a neon sign above her head announcing she was a newcomer. She whispered a quick prayer for the service to start early.

Finally the organ bellowed and a man at the front asked the congregation to stand for opening prayer. As they did, Emily noticed several people her age slip into the pew in front of her. They had to be college students. She tried to focus on the pastor's message, but Emily kept imagining different scenarios where those students turned around, introduced themselves, and warmly welcomed her into their group, inviting her to join them for Bible study, lunch, a movie, anything. Sadly, Emily was forced to abandon her favorite of these daydreams—the one where her new friends throw her a surprise birthday party and tell her how glad they are she came to Seattle—when everyone suddenly stood to sing the closing hymn. It was a good thing Emily knew this one by heart, because she was much too preoccupied with her imaginary friends to pay much attention to the music.

Emily took her time returning her hymnal to the rack in front of her and pretended to fumble for her keys as she waited for someone to approach her, but it didn't happen. The group in front of her made their way quickly outside, arguing as they exited over whether or not they should go to Denny's for brunch. Once they were gone, Emily decided she might as well head for the door, too.

As she headed back to McNeil Hall, Emily silently fumed. *What kind of church was that? No one even spoke to me the whole time I was there and they call themselves Christians? That would never happen at our church!* Or would it? Emily suddenly remembered many Sundays spent huddled together with her own familiar group of friends, discussing plans for after church. She liked to think they would reach out to someone new, but how often had they invited someone not in their circle to join them? Not very often, Emily sadly concluded.

Okay, God, I'm sorry I haven't always been as nice to new people as I should be, but can't we just put that behind us? It won't happen again. In the meantime, here I am hundreds of miles from home, deserted by my best friend, and no one has even spoken to me for more than twelve hours. If you could just help me make a friend, one measly friend, I would be eternally grateful.

When she entered her room, Emily was wondering if she'd be able to survive another twenty-four hours like the last. She was so eager for human contact, Emily even felt happy to see Cooper, who was busy digging through her desk drawer and shoving random items into a black backpack. She didn't notice Emily come in, so when she finally did look up, she jumped in surprise. "Don't scare me like that!" she said accusingly.

Emily was so stunned by the unfairness of the statement that she had trouble thinking of an appropriate response. Cooper, of course, regained her composure more quickly.

"Sorry. I didn't hear you come in. I'm not usually coherent at this hour, but I'm meeting my Aunt Penny for breakfast. I'm already late and I still have to drive all the way to Redmond, so I guess I'll see you later."

As Cooper raced out the door, Emily glanced at her watch. It was 10:30. *What kind of person isn't usually coherent at 10:30 in the morning?* Maybe it was best not to waste her time trying to figure Cooper out, she decided with a shrug.

Hoping to find Kenzie in, Emily wandered into their shared living room and plopped down on the couch with her copy of the orientation schedule in one hand and a Cherry Coke in the other. She had popped a cassette into her tape player and was reading about the outdoor movie being shown on the back of the gym that night when Kenzie came in, all dressed up and carrying a Bible under her arm.

Emily's heart leapt. *Kenzie's a Christian!* She had a feeling she and Kenzie were going to become good friends when they met the day before, and now she was sure of it. Emily forced herself to sound casual as she asked Kenzie if she had just come from church.

"Yeah, an old college friend of my dad's is on staff at a church downtown, so we went to an early service there and out to breakfast before my folks' plane left," Kenzie explained.

Just as Emily asked Kenzie if she planned to continue

attending there or find a church closer to campus, music from Emily's room filled the living area, drowning out her response. Emily was so glad to see a friendly face that she hadn't noticed the tape had come to an end until the auto-reverse kicked in.

Emily returned to her own room to adjust the volume. She was only gone a few seconds, but when she came back Kenzie seemed changed. Emily attempted to draw her into a conversation about the song they were listening to.

"You should hear it done live!" Emily exclaimed. She began to tell Kenzie about the artist's concert, which she had attended the previous year, but Kenzie only listened politely. As soon as Emily finished her story, her suite-mate excused herself to make a phone call. Emily had no idea why Kenzie was suddenly cool toward her just when they seemed to be getting along so well.

I wonder if I'll ever understand anyone here at college, Emily thought as she stared at Kenzie's closed door.

Just when Emily was convinced she would never make any friends at PCU, there was a knock at the door. The way things were going, Emily wasn't sure she should answer it. What she really wanted to do was get into bed and pull the covers up over her head, but she knew that wouldn't help her adjust to college life any faster. When she tentatively opened the door, a petite blonde with short cropped hair stood smiling on the other side.

"Hi, is Emily here?" the girl inquired.

"That's me," Emily answered hesitantly, wondering if, for some reason, she should know this person.

"I'm Zoey Criswell. Lisa, our R.A., passed out lists of all the orientation groups last night and it looks like you and I are the only ones from this floor in the same group. Since I didn't run into you at the ice-cream social, I thought I'd come see if you wanted to grab some lunch before the meeting." Zoey hesitated. "I mean, if you don't already have other plans, that is."

"No, I don't have any other plans," Emily admitted, glad Cooper had explained the whole "R.A." thing to her so she knew what Zoey was talking about. "And I'd love to have some company for lunch. Let me just grab my ID card."

As she and Zoey made their way across campus to the cafeteria, Emily found herself humming the "Hallelujah Chorus" under her breath.

Well, at least your roommate is from this planet!" Emily said, laughing, when Zoey had finished recounting her own experience moving into the dorm and meeting her roommate, Clarissa.

"Let's see if you still feel that way after you meet her."

"But you must have met some people at the party last night," Emily insisted. "Wasn't there anyone normal there?"

Zoey shook her head. "I have never felt like such a reject in my life. No one but our R.A. talked to me. I started to think maybe I had hot fudge on my face or something, but when I caught my reflection in one of the lounge windows I looked fine. Still, it was sheer torture. Be glad you didn't come."

"It's nice to know someone else is having a tough time connecting with people," Emily confessed. "I was beginning to think it was just me."

"Oh, no," Zoey assured her, then added with a conspiratorial wink, "It's everyone else. *We're* the normal ones."

It turned out that the girls had a great deal in common. Both had been on their high school track teams and both craved junk food. They loved the outdoors and Zoey was even from the

Portland area. In fact, when Emily described where her family used to live, Zoey knew exactly where their old neighborhood was. The two made their way through the cafeteria line, piling food on their orange trays as they continued to compare notes. They kept talking clear through lunch, and by the time they had finished their mediocre tacos, the relationship was solidified.

After dumping their trash and stacking their trays, the two girls headed off for their first official meeting as freshmen.

"So what do you think these orientation groups are going to be like?" Emily asked her new friend.

"Well, the official reason for them is to make sure each freshman has an opportunity to meet other freshmen, and to help new students adjust to college life. But I heard the real purpose is to keep us all so busy we don't have time to call home and tell our parents how miserable we are."

Emily raised an arched brow at Zoey. She hadn't been able to get half this much information from her brother, the orientation leader, during their almost seven hour trip to college. Already, this new friend was proving to be a valuable resource.

"Since they're mandatory, I guess it doesn't much matter, but I hope they're at least a little fun," Emily said.

Just then, they turned the corner and the ivy-covered administration building came into view. Zoey and Emily turned to stare at each other, their mouths both forming the word "Wow!" at exactly the same time. The lawn was already filled with several hundred students, clustered in groups around huge signs numbered one to twenty-five. The girls quickly located the sign for Group 16, but the throngs of people made it almost impossible for them to reach their meeting area on the far side of the quad.

After pushing their way past a hundred or so freshmen and almost getting tackled when they unknowingly stumbled into a game of tag, Emily and Zoey stood triumphantly on the administration building's front steps and tried to catch their breath. Before the girls were able to recover fully, a gorgeous guy with sun-bleached hair, a deep tan, and liquid blue eyes approached them.

"Hi, I'm Nick Carrera, Group 16's orientation leader. Are you girls mine?"

Emily started to say yes when Zoey chimed in. "I'm definitely yours," she said with a big smile which Nick easily returned.

Emily just stared. She could never say anything like that to a guy. *Maybe that's why I've never had a serious boyfriend.* Before she could give it any more thought, Zoey was dragging her closer to the sign with the big 16 painted on it.

Nick gathered the other members of Group 16 together and began shouting over the noise. "I need all of you to follow me over to the student union building where it's a little more quiet so we can get started."

They all obliged, looking a bit like baby ducklings as they huddled close and followed their leader across campus. Once inside the building, they plopped down on the couches in the lounge.

"Welcome to the SUB," Nick said, explaining that on campus everyone referred to the student union building that way. Emily added it to her mental list of acronyms to remember as Nick pulled out a folder and started reading off names.

"Sorry to be make you feel like you're back in elementary school here, but rules are rules and hey, it's an easy unit," he explained, referring to the class credit each student would get for attending the class.

Zoey was first, followed by a guy named Dan who had long, dark, curly hair pulled back into a ponytail and even darker glasses hiding his eyes. He looked bored already, in contrast to the three enthusiastic girls whose names were called next. The girls all looked alike, Emily noticed, not so much like sisters, but as if they all shopped at the same place, and they all wore the same adoring expression when they looked at Nick. Next was a studious, overdressed boy named Steve, then Emily, and finally, a guy named John Wehmeyer, who appeared to be a slightly less gorgeous version of Nick.

John had short brown hair and icy-blue eyes that Emily thought were incredible, even half-hidden by the bill of his Dodger's cap. After studying him for a few seconds, she forced herself to look away, knowing that she wouldn't be able to stop herself from blushing if she caught his eye.

"Now that we've established that everyone from Group 16 is present and accounted for, why don't we go around the room and each give our vital stats—hometown, major if you've decided, what dorm you're assigned to, hobbies, and anything else we might find interesting. I promise it will be relatively painless," Nick said.

Emily hoped she wouldn't have to go first and was relieved when Nick's gaze rested on Zoey. Her new friend had no trouble rattling off the requested information and even added a few extra bits of news about herself. The others didn't volunteer any more than was asked and Emily did the same. Finally, it was John's turn. Emily hoped her interest wasn't too obvious, but when Zoey nudged her and gave her a knowing look, she knew she'd been found out and felt her cheeks turn bright pink.

John was from Mission Viejo, which he explained was in

Southern California, "about thirty minutes south of Disney-land," and he planned to study marketing. He hoped to work for a big ad agency eventually, creating television commercials. "My hobbies include hiking and beach volleyball, and this summer I learned to water-ski with my youth group," he finished in a deep game-show host voice, before breaking into a warm smile.

Youth group! John was a Christian, too! But before Emily had time to ponder this information further, Nick began running down the list of activities scheduled for the week.

"In keeping with oh-so-festive nautical theme we'll be watching *The Hunt for Red October* on the outside wall of the gym tonight, then taking a harbor cruise around Seattle on Monday. And Tuesday night, after you guys have spent hours and hours in long registration lines—I'm not exaggerating here —you will have earned an evening at the ballpark, so the entire freshman class is going to a Seattle Mariner's game."

A cheer erupted from Group 16.

"But wait, there's more," Nick said with a grin. "Wednesday we'll meet up again for what I like to call 'the big anti-drinking-how-to-be-sexually-responsible talk,' which really isn't as bad as it sounds. The administration just wants us to let you know what university policy is on stuff like underage drinking, sexual harassment, hazing, et cetera, and to make sure you're prepared for some of the issues you'll face now that you're in college. "

Emily was glad there would be plenty to occupy her time until classes began on Thursday.

"That's our last introductory meeting," Nick said. "But don't start missing me yet. We'll still meet once a week for the first eight weeks of the semester to see how you're all doing. Hey, you have to do something to earn that credit and I'll try my best to make it fun whenever I can. We can share studying tips and talk about any roommate problems. I might even let you guys in on a valuable secret or two like where to find the spiciest burritos in Seattle or which movie theater in town has the best popcorn. We'll just have to wait and see."

With all the important announcements taken care of, it was time for the games portion of the meeting, which Nick immediately began to explain.

"At the risk of overdoing that whole nautical thing, we're sending you new recruits on a little treasure hunt. Just think of it as our creative way of helping you learn your way around campus."

The eight group members groaned as they got to their feet, stretched their legs, and gathered up their belongings. Undaunted, their fearless leader read through the list of names again, this time pairing up people for the competition.

He was halfway through before Emily realized she would be on John's team. She turned to Zoey with a horrified look on her face, but her friend just smiled slyly. Realizing she would get no sympathy there, Emily turned to grab one of the sheets of paper that detailed the items they would need to find. As she spun around, Emily walked right into John. As if that wasn't bad enough, the collision caused her to lose her balance, and she was forced to grab his sleeve to steady herself.

So much for making a good impression.

6

Emily wished she could crawl into a hole, but John took the whole thing in stride. While she was still gripping the sleeve of his denim shirt, he grabbed her free arm and spun her around, saying, "Why, yes, I'd love to dance, Miss Stewart."

As he twirled her a final time, he pulled her in close to his chest. Emily realized that her head was spinning, too, but she was pretty sure it wasn't from losing her balance. *And he knew my last name!* she thought, trying to hide the huge grin that involuntarily spread across her face. She was still a little light-headed as they struck out in search of the student health center, where they were to "borrow" a tongue depressor.

According to the map Nick had given them, John and Emily would need to walk all the way around campus to get to the health center, following University Drive as it curved toward the school's entrance. But John insisted he knew a shortcut. He did, however, fail to mention it would require scaling a six-foot-high brick wall.

"Oh, you know a shortcut, do you?" Emily teased, eyeing the roadblock.

"What's the problem? You don't look the kind of girl who

would let a tiny little wall stand in her way," John shot back.

Emily had always found it impossible to resist a challenge, so she got a running start, jumped up and grabbed the top of the wall, and swung her right leg over. From there she found it easy to pull herself up to a sitting position before lowering herself down to the ground.

"I could have given you a boost," John said, when he reached the other side himself, but he was clearly impressed that petite Emily hadn't needed his help. As they crossed through the medical center parking lot he reached up and removed a small dried leaf that was tangled in her hair, then handed it to her as they reached their first destination.

While John was busy explaining why they needed the tongue depressor to the student nurse on duty, Emily tucked the leaf carefully in her pocket and consulted the list to see where they were headed next.

"We're off to the computer lab," Emily told John when he returned with the wooden stick. Their search also included the science hall, research center in the library, tutoring center, post office, bookstore, and campus radio station. Out of breath and with their hands and pockets full, they returned to the SUB. All they needed now was a flyer from the events board on the second floor. Emily found one for a concert downtown and ripped it from the board. Triumphant, she and John returned to the group's meeting place and dumped their treasures on the coffee table Nick was using for a footrest.

"Looks like you guys were quite successful," he said admiringly.

Before they could respond, Zoey and Dan returned, laughing hysterically. Emily regarded them with surprise. Was this the same Dan who trudged off an hour earlier, complaining about "these stupid childish games" and mumbling "I knew I should have gone to community college"? The other two groups returned soon thereafter, and everyone gathered around as Nick checked off each item before declaring John and Emily the official winners.

"Now while I'm sure you feel the knowledge you gained on this little quest is prize enough, I also have two coupons for a free frozen yogurt at The Shack, PCU's own snack bar, for the victors…because that's just the kind of guy I am," Nick announced, handing John and Emily each a bright pink slip of paper.

"And with that, you're free to go," their leader said, by way of dismissal. "But don't forget, the cafeteria is open for dinner from five to seven, and the movie starts at eight."

Emily was almost out the door when she felt a hand on her shoulder. It was John, holding the blue PCU sweatshirt Ryan had given her last Christmas. "I think this is yours," he said, handing it to her. "You left it on the couch back there."

Emily thanked him and attempted to leave once more. She had gone only a few feet before she heard him yell, "Hope I see you at the movie tonight, *partner*."

She walked outside, clutching her sweatshirt tightly. Emily had gone several yards before she noticed her friend at her side. It took the sound of Zoey's voice to bring her back to earth.

"Oh, that was really smooth," Zoey said.

"What was?" Emily looked around, thinking maybe she had missed something while replaying the afternoon's events in her head.

"You know, the way you 'accidentally' left your sweatshirt

behind," Zoey explained, nudging Emily knowingly. "I wish I had thought of it. But then again, I don't think Nick would have come running after me the way John ran after you."

"But it was an accident!" Emily protested. "I really did forget my sweatshirt."

"Oh please! Next you're going to tell me you didn't even notice the way John was looking at you when we left."

"He was looking at me?" Emily asked hopefully.

"Stewart, you are hopeless," Zoey said, shaking her head.

The girls walked a while in silence, before Zoey asked again, "You mean you really didn't plan that?" She sounded genuinely surprised.

"No, of course not," Emily answered, sounding a little offended. "I'm never able to think of stuff like that anyway. But if it makes you feel any better, I will admit that I do think John is really cute."

"Well, I had a hard time prying my eyes away from Nick," Zoey confessed. "But yeah, John is pretty cute. And for what it's worth, I think he likes you."

Emily felt a warm glow spread through her at Zoey's words, and she couldn't help but marvel at how much things had changed since that morning. *I think I might just like it here after all,* she thought as she pulled the crumpled leaf John had given her out of her pocket and held it tight.

7

The suite was empty when Emily returned. Apparently, Cooper and Kenzie were still with their orientation groups. Emily realized that, oddly, she didn't even know if she had a third suite-mate. It didn't seem likely; she hadn't noticed anyone else moving in. And if Kenzie did have a roommate, Emily certainly would have run into her by now, wouldn't she?

Spotting the letter to Holly on her desk, Emily grabbed it and crumpled it into a ball before throwing it into the trash can. So much had changed since last night. Taking out a clean sheet of paper, she poured out the details of the last few hours. Emily also included a detailed description of Cooper and Kenzie, adding how they only made her miss Holly more. Then she sealed the envelope and leaned back in her desk chair with a satisfied sigh before curling up for a nap.

A few hours later, Zoey was at Emily's door again.

"Wanna grab some dinner before the movie?"

"Sure," Emily replied.

"You better grab something to sit on."

An hour later, the girls sat on thick beach towels spread out upon the lawn behind the gym while they waited for the movie to start. The grassy field was definitely damp, and they were glad they had thought ahead. As they waited for the movie to start, they looked wistfully at the big bag of cheddar cheese popcorn the girls next to them had brought. Dinner that night had been less than wonderful. Both Emily and Zoey had left most of their lasagna and were forced to fill up on salad and garlic bread.

"What I wouldn't give for a package of chocolate covered peanuts!" Emily whispered to Zoey.

"I was craving Red Vines myself," Zoey answered.

"Oh, no. It has to be some form of chocolate, or it just isn't worth the calories," Emily explained emphatically.

Before Zoey could protest, John and Dan appeared. Emily was surprised to see them together since they seemed so different, but then she remembered they both lived in Maury Hall.

"Mind if we join you?" John asked. He plopped down on Emily's towel before either of the girls had a chance to answer. Dan looked a little more hesitant. Even though he and Zoey had gotten along great during the scavenger hunt, it seemed that he didn't want to just assume there was a friendship there.

Maybe he was just acting bored earlier because he's really shy, Emily thought. Giving him the benefit of the doubt, she smiled up at him encouragingly.

"There's room right here between Zoey and me," she said, scooting closer to John.

Once they were all situated, John reached inside his jacket. "We can't be expected to enjoy a movie without a little chocolate now can we?" He pulled out a big bag of peanut M&Ms, which he passed around.

Zoey gave Emily a knowing smile and popped a few of the

candies in her mouth. "They're not Red Vines, but I guess they'll do," she said, chomping away.

Just then the movie lights flickered, and cheers erupted from the rowdy crowd. Emily had never seen the movie before, but she knew she would love the suspenseful story line. In fact, almost everyone seemed to be drawn in and the crowd had quieted down by the time the opening credits were finished.

In order to fit on the towels, their small group had to sit pretty close together, so Emily was shoulder-to-shoulder with John throughout the entire movie. Although she willed the film not to end, eventually the closing credits rolled. Just when Emily thought she'd have to say good-bye to John, an orientation leader with a red bullhorn stood to introduce another video.

"Now, I know you guys have been lounging around the pool all summer and probably haven't cracked a book since June, so we've planned a little refresher course," explained an athletic looking girl, wearing a Patagonia jacket, jeans, and Birkenstocks.

Several "Schoolhouse Rock" clips followed. Emily vaguely remembered the animated educational spots that used to air on Saturday mornings between her favorite cartoons. This selection proved to be a huge hit with the PCU freshman class, with everyone joining in on the choruses of "Conjunction Junction" and "I'm Just a Bill." People were still singing long after the back wall of the gym went dark and the crowd had begun to walk off into the night.

John and Dan walked with the girls for awhile before turning toward their own dorm. Emily and Zoey continued in companionable silence. When they reached her door, Emily turned to her new friend.

51

"Thanks for going with me tonight. It was really fun," she said, then hesitated a moment before adding, "I can't believe we just met this morning. I feel like I've known you for years."

"Me, too," Zoey agreed.

"Thanks for knocking on my door. I don't know what I would have done if we hadn't met."

"Luckily, we don't have to find out," Zoey said with a smile.

After making plans to meet for an early morning jog, the girls parted company. Emily made her way through the suite living room, stopping to grab a drink from the fridge, then deposited her dirty beach towel into the laundry basket on the floor of her closet. As she tossed her keys on her desk, Emily's eyes grew large.

Everything Cooper had put away yesterday was back out.

All the clothes that had been in drawers that morning now covered the floor, and several empty Perrier bottles littered the desk. The black shelf, which yesterday had been home only to Cooper's stereo, now sported a lacy white bra hanging from one corner, two open packages of rice cakes, several bottles of nail polish, and a small plastic container which, upon closer inspection, Emily found to be filled with cloudy water. Several tiny, opened envelopes partially covered a colorful pamphlet with the words "Grow Your Own Sea-Monkeys" printed on the front. Emily remembered that her little brother Josh had some a few years ago, but they never grew to look anything like the surreal creatures on the package.

Sea-Monkeys? I don't even think we're supposed to have fish! And why would Cooper want them? Doesn't she know they're only brine shrimp? Even if they are allowed, I don't think Cooper is someone who should be allowed to keep containers of water near electri-

cal appliances. It's only a matter of time before she gets herself elec-trocuted.

Just then Cooper and Kenzie burst into the suite, paper Starbucks cups in hand.

"We went out for a latté," Kenzie explained, holding up her cup for closer inspection. "Were you at the movie?"

"Yeah, I just got back," Emily answered, glad that Kenzie was being friendly again, even if her own roommate had yet to offer so much as a "Hi."

Kenzie crossed the room to the bookshelf where Emily stood and peered into the tiny Sea-Monkey tank.

"And these would be…?"

"A going away present," Cooper explained reluctantly, grab-bing the bra from the shelf and tossing it onto the bed. "My friend Claire gave them to me before I left New York. She knew I was going to miss Winston Churchill—that's my bulldog—so she gave me the Sea-Monkeys to keep me company. I tried to say no, but the alternative was an ant farm, and that would have been worse. I just know I would have dropped it eventu-ally and the ants would have gotten loose."

"Thank you for opting for the Sea-Monkeys, then," Emily said. She didn't mind bugs in the great outdoors, but the thought of the little black creatures crawling around their room made her shiver.

"No problem," Cooper answered, as she turned on the blinking stoplight and cranked up her stereo. "You don't mind a little music, do you?"

Emily did mind. But she didn't want to give Cooper any valid reason to dislike her, so she kept her thoughts to herself. Kenzie said good-night and left for her own room. While the music blared, Cooper sang off-key and cleared a space on her bed to sleep. Emily watched her roommate stack a number of items precariously on her desk. Putting her clothes away and tucking her shoes neatly under the bed, Emily wondered how they would ever last nine months together.

The room didn't look any better in the morning, but a three-mile run with Zoey helped Emily forget the mess for awhile. When they finished, Emily was dying for a shower, but Zoey convinced her to stop at the cafeteria for some breakfast first.

"Come on. It's just a little sweat. No one will be in there this early anyway," she pleaded.

Emily grudgingly agreed, and Zoey was right. The cafeteria was all but deserted, and the girls walked right in without waiting in the usual line. After loading their trays up with pancakes, scrambled eggs, bacon, and sausage, they headed for a corner table.

"It's a good thing no one's here. I am being a total pig, but I really worked up an appetite," Emily said.

Zoey nodded in agreement, her mouth full of pancake. Just as Emily took a bite, she saw her friend's eyes grow wide as her gaze focused on something over Emily's shoulder. Somehow, Emily knew what was wrong before she even turned around. As she tried quickly to swallow, John set down his tray.

"Hope I'm not interrupting anything," he said with a smile.

"Of course not," Emily replied, glaring at Zoey as she wiped her sweaty forehead with her sleeve. "We were just having a little breakfast."

"That's an understatement," John said, taking in the contents of the girls' trays.

Emily forced a smile. *At least he didn't comment on our appearance,* she thought.

"Hey, where'd you get that Cap'n Crunch?" Zoey asked, watching John shovel crunchberries into his mouth.

"It's at the cereal bar around the corner. Dan discovered it on Saturday night, and it's been a lifesaver. If I had to survive on the regular food they serve, I would be hospitalized for malnutrition before Thanksgiving break for sure. Now when I don't like what they're having—which is always—I have a back-up. I've been averaging two bowls at every meal."

Cereal sounded really good, but Emily wasn't about to add anything else to her overflowing tray with John there. She made a mental note to remember at lunch, though.

"Ranch dressing is another little secret," John confided. "They hide it over there at the condiment bar. If you put it on the French fries, you hardly notice how soggy they are."

"Apparently we didn't explore the cafeteria fully, Zoey."

"It's a good thing you have me around then, isn't it?" John asked.

Emily just smiled. The rest of the meal was uneventful, and they parted with a promise to see each other on the bay cruise.

That afternoon, Emily spent two glorious hours sitting with John on the boat, tossing questions back and forth. In the distance, the Space Needle rose from Seattle's beautiful skyline.

The view was wasted on Emily, though. All Emily noticed was how John's hair glinted in the sun as they told each other about their families, their home churches, and their reasons for coming to PCU.

John had been attending his current church only since June, Emily found out. "I went on the water-ski trip with a friend from high school, then just sort of stuck around," he explained. He added, "They had a lot more going on than the last church I went to."

John teased Emily about being a pastor's kid after she told him about her family, and Emily managed to find out that John had one younger brother who was thirteen. He also told her that his parents were divorced and that he lived with his mom and stepdad, who had married when John was in junior high. When Emily asked John if his dad lived in Mission Viejo, too, he quickly changed the subject. He was easy to talk to about everything else, though. And despite their different upbringings they had a lot in common, especially their love of the outdoors and anything athletic, not to mention their shared passion for chocolate. The afternoon was everything Emily could have hoped.

Emily was at Zoey's door bright and early Tuesday morning, having left her own room before Cooper even opened her eyes. "Ready to brave the registration lines?" she asked enthusiastically.

"Your good mood wouldn't have anything to do with a certain guy we both know, now would it?" Zoey grinned.

They talked about John all the way to the administration building. But Emily's mood wasn't quite so light after they had waited in line for hours only to find out they couldn't get into any of their first-choice classes. With a lot of juggling, though, each girl finally ended up with something resembling a schedule. The line to buy books was even worse, and when they finally reached the window, the frazzled girls were asked questions they couldn't possibly answer.

"Do you want new or used books?"

"Optional materials or just the required texts?"

"We're out of fourth editions. Will a third edition do?"

"Do you need the syllabus, too?"

Emily wasn't sure she even knew what a syllabus was. In the end, not wanting to stand in that line again, they bought everything offered to them and lugged the stacks of books back to their rooms.

"Come get me when you leave for the baseball game," Zoey instructed as she staggered down the hall with her arms full.

At the Kingdome that night, everyone in Group 16 had a great time. Even "the triplets," as Zoey and Emily had started referring to the other three girls in their group, loosened up a little. John sat next to Emily, and Zoey, in what she saw as a major coup, managed to snag the seat next to Nick.

Neither girl had ever been to a professional baseball game before, so it was especially exciting. They bought bags of peanuts from a vendor walking up and down the rows, then spent the next half hour covering the area around them with shells. During the seventh inning stretch, they climbed up on their seats and loudly sang "Take Me Out to the Ballgame" even though neither one of them knew all the words. They finally had to sit back down after they began laughing so hard they almost fell into the row behind them.

Emily was still laughing when John leaned over and whispered, "I take it you're having fun at your first baseball game."

"How can you tell?"

"By all the food you've spilled on yourself," he explained, picking a piece of shell off her shirt.

Emily looked down the front of her. Sure enough, her clothes were dotted with salt and peanut shells. She began to brush at them as she spoke.

"It's funny, I always thought it was kind of boring watching it on television, but it's so much better live."

"They're even better when they're outdoors and not played on Astroturf. You haven't lived until you've seen a game at Dodger Stadium."

"I'm sure you're right, but I don't get to Southern California much," Emily explained.

"Well, maybe now you'll have more of a reason to go," John suggested.

"Maybe," Emily replied thoughtfully, wondering if it was the Dodgers or himself he was referring to. She slid down in her seat and crossed her arms over her dirty shirt.

Later that night, they sleepily boarded the bus that would take them back to campus, and Emily slid in beside Zoey without a second thought. John stopped short and gave her a funny look before settling into a seat across the aisle. Emily tried to shrug it off as she leaned her head back against the bus seat and closed her eyes. She was exhausted, and if she was going to fall asleep on someone's shoulder she would rather it be Zoey's. If she accidentally began to drool she didn't want to be sitting next to John, but she could hardly explain that to him.

When Zoey woke her, they were in front of the SUB and the bus was half-empty. As she made her way down the narrow aisle, Emily noticed John's seat was already vacant.

He hadn't even waited to say good-bye.

On the way to their orientation meeting the next day, Emily quizzed Zoey about John's behavior.

"I may not have a lot of experience in this area," Emily admitted, "but John seemed like he was interested. Everything was going really well until the ride home last night. What happened?"

"Well, I like to think I *have* quite a bit of experience in this area," Zoey proclaimed, "and I think he was just being a guy. He expected you to sit with him and was mad when you didn't. Maybe he was going to ask you out on the ride home or something and you ruined his plan. He might have thought you were trying to blow him off."

"You know I wasn't!" Emily cried.

"Unfortunately, I'm not the one you have to convince. If I were you, I'd do whatever I could today to let him know I was still interested."

Emily was extremely nervous when they entered the Student Union Building. She thought it had been clear to John that she liked him. They'd sat next to each other throughout the entire game and had spent hours on the boat together the day before. She didn't know liking someone meant having to be together every minute, and if it did, was that what she wanted? Things seemed to be moving so fast.

With her heart beating frantically, Emily scanned the faces in the lounge until her eyes found John. He was talking to one of the triplets, leaning close to hear what she was saying. Emily thought he saw her out of the corner of his eye, but couldn't be sure. In any case, he made no move to join her.

"Have a seat," Zoey said sympathetically, patting the spot next to her on the couch. Emily planted herself next to Zoey, glad they didn't have to wait long for the meeting to start. As Nick called things to order he pulled out a stack of pamphlets and began passing them around. Emily studied the front of one —a collage of beer bottles, pills, and syringes. The other was titled "Everything You Need to Know about Birth Control and STDs."

Emily remembered seeing this type of pamphlet in her high school health class when they had covered the unit on drinking, drugs, and sex. At the time she had tuned out. After all, none of her friends had ever tried drugs that she knew of. She couldn't go to school dances until she was seventeen, so she hadn't been exposed to alcohol all that much, either. Since their town was so small, kids weren't really able to have big parties with kegs of beer because parents always found out. And Emily knew she wasn't going to have sex until she was married, so what was there to talk about? She prepared to tune out again. But then Nick got started.

"I have to give you this stuff because the administration told me to, but let's be honest. I know you're not gonna read it. I didn't read it last year when they gave it to me, either."

Emily couldn't believe her ears. In high school, they at least had to cover the information.

"College is an important time of experimentation, and the administration knows that as well as anyone," Nick went on. "Now, the official party line is that PCU is a 'dry' campus, which means alcohol of any kind is not permitted. In order to avoid lawsuits, the university needs to let you know that under-age drinking is not permitted off campus in the fraternity and sorority houses, either," he continued. "But everyone knows drinking goes on, so let me tell you what you really want to know—how to not get caught. First off, it's not cool to keep beer in your dorm rooms. Next, if you use a fake ID to get into the local bars, make sure it's a good one. The bouncers know what out-of-state licenses look like and those things you send away for in the back of magazines are a dead giveaway."

Emily hoped no one noticed the shocked look on her face. She knew people did dishonest things like using fake IDs; it was just weird to hear Nick, who was supposed to be a role model, condone it. *I must have misunderstood,* Emily thought, turning her focus back to Nick's talk.

"Now, at the frat houses, beware of the punch. You never know what kind of alcohol is in it, so if you aren't used to drinking, take it slow. I can't tell you how many freshmen I've seen hugging the toilet on Friday and Saturday nights. It's not a pretty sight. Oh, and I'd also avoid any baked goods at a party. People who have no clue what they're doing have been known to stick marijuana or even heroin into brownies, or anything else they can find, and that always leads to trouble."

Emily tried to imagine her brother giving a similar speech to his orientation group, but she couldn't.

"Now for the sex talk," Nick began, adding quickly, "Wow, I feel like a parent."

Most of the group laughed a little nervously. Emily found it weird to be talking about this subject with people she'd just met. At least in high school sex ed, they'd had class together all semester first. Emily doubted the talk Nick was about to give on the subject would be anything like the one she had with her parents several years ago.

"Basically, the administration just wants me to warn you to be careful," Nick was saying. "A lot of people go a little crazy when they're away from home for the first time, which is okay as long as you're safe. But don't believe anyone who tells you that you can't catch anything. There are a lot of sexually transmitted diseases out there, and I'm not just talking about AIDS. You can get free condoms in the student health center, so there's no excuse. And if I were you guys I'd work out a system now with your roommates about members of the opposite sex sleeping over. Set some basic ground rules so you don't wake up one morning and find you have company only after you've just come out of the shower wearing nothing but a towel."

Nick continued to talk for another five to ten minutes, but Emily had a hard time focusing on what he said. She was so overwhelmed after the meeting that she completely forgot about John. She and Zoey went to the post office to check their mailboxes, which of course were empty, then headed home. As they walked, Zoey commented a few times on how cool she thought Nick was. She thought it was refreshing to hear someone talk honestly about all that stuff instead of the way most adults handled it, pretending it wasn't going on.

Emily was caught up in her thoughts, still busy processing what Nick had told them. She was about to absent-mindedly agree with her friend, but then what Zoey had said began to sink in.

"You know, Zoey, I didn't think it was cool at all," Emily said calmly. "I like Nick, but I think he was wrong to say drinking was okay as long as we're responsible. If we're under twenty-one, it's illegal; so tell me, how can we break the law responsibly? Not only that, I read an article in a magazine last summer about a girl our age who died from something called alcohol poisoning. She went to a party and was drinking beer then switched to shots of tequila. Finally, she drank so much, her system just shut down."

"That sounds like a pretty extreme case. But, look, you don't have to worry about me, I don't drink anyway," Zoey said.

"Neither do I, but that's just part of what bothered me. It seems like Nick was just expecting the worst from all of us. As if everyone goes off the deep end when they get to college. He talked about condoms and all that like they make it okay to have sex, but he didn't say anything about love or commitment or why you might not want to have sex yet," Emily finished, taking a deep breath.

"I think he was just being realistic," Zoey insisted. "Maybe most freshmen do drink and have sex."

"Or maybe you just think they do because people like Nick lead you to believe that's the norm," Emily countered.

"I don't know," Zoey said, raising her hands in surrender. "Why are we arguing about this anyway?"

"I don't remember," Emily answered, truthfully.

"Well, then, I'm going to my room. I promised my parents

I'd call them tonight. Besides, we have a big day tomorrow— first day of class!"

Emily gave her friend a halfhearted wave before wandering back to her room, the afternoon's events still gnawing at her.

10

Thursday morning dawned gray and rainy, ending Seattle's uncharacteristic stretch of sunshine. The weather matched Emily's gray mood, though. John was acting strange, Nick had disappointed her, it looked like she and Zoey might not have as much in common as she first thought, and her roommate was a total slob.

As Emily looked over at Cooper, buried under not only her blankets but also several layers of stray clothing, she recalled Nick's words. *I can't*, she thought. *I just can't ask Cooper if she plans on bringing guys back to our room. I would die of embarrassment and even worse, what if she says yes?* For the millionth time Emily wished Holly had come to college with her, but since wishing wasn't going to make that happen, she grabbed her robe and headed for the shower.

Thirty minutes later, Emily pulled on a red canvas jacket to protect her from the rain and consulted her schedule one more time before leaving for her first class, U.S. History. At least she knew her way around the beautiful old campus thanks to that scavenger hunt. When she first arrived at school, Emily didn't think she'd ever be able to tell the ivy-covered brick buildings apart. Now, just a few days later, she felt confident that she could find her way to Ward Hall, room 101. It was a good thing because class started in just ten minutes.

She entered the cavernous lecture hall and stopped for a minute to take it all in. Emily had never seen such a huge classroom. Instead of desks, the room was filled with several hundred seats, giving it the look and feel of a movie theater. Emily found her way to one of the middle rows and, once seated, pulled out a notebook, pen, and the two-inch thick document they had sold her at the bookstore, which she could only assume was a syllabus.

At exactly 9:00 A.M., a gray-haired man approached the podium in the front of the room and introduced himself as Professor Holden. Emily's college career was underway. The syllabus, she soon found out, was just one long two-hundred-page outline. During each class the teacher would lecture; the students were expected to listen and fill in the missing information in the syllabus, which they would then use to study for exams. It was all beginning to make sense.

Since it was the first day, much time was taken up going over details like the attendance policy (no more than six absences were permitted, students were to sign in at the door), exam dates (there would be three and yes, they were comprehensive), and grading (the word "curve" was, apparently, not in Professor Holden's vocabulary). There would also be weekly quizzes. With that taken care of and only ten minutes left of the class period, the students assumed they would be excused early. The noise level rose accordingly as students unzipped backpacks and stowed books, but they were mistaken.

Without contradicting them verbally, Professor Holden

turned to page one in his copy of the syllabus and began lecturing. As he spoke firmly into the microphone, his point was made. This was his class and it was over when he said it was. Clearly, no one would be getting a free ride in U.S. History.

The day got better from there. Emily had thirty minutes before English Lit, so she stopped off at The Shack and grabbed a carton of chocolate milk. As she drank her breakfast on the way to her next class, she thought of the coupons for free frozen yogurt she and John had won and wondered if they would get to use them together. She doubted it. Now that classes were in full swing, with all the upperclassmen back on PCU's now-crowded campus, running into John didn't seem nearly as likely as it had earlier in the week.

As Emily entered her English Literature classroom, she felt instantly relieved. From the front, Garfield Hall looked like a carbon copy of Ward Hall with wings, but once inside she found that room 216 was small, filled with only twenty or so desks, and looked like a composite of all the classrooms she had ever been in. Emily sat near the front and pulled out the used copy of Jane Austen's *Pride and Prejudice* that had been the only required text listed for the class.

Ah, no syllabus. I like this class already, Emily thought with a satisfied smile. Just as she looked up from thumbing through the novel, she saw John enter the room. He seemed a little unsure of what to do, but when Emily smiled he quickly took the seat next to her.

"I can't believe I got stuck with English Lit. It's so much harder than American Lit. I don't know how I'll make it through," John complained.

"I wasn't too thrilled when they told me the other class was full, either. But this book looks pretty good. Anyway, English is my best subject so if you want, maybe we can study together?" Emily offered, hoping this was what Zoey had in mind when she counseled Emily to make her interest clear.

"That would be great." John seemed to brighten up. "Even if the book isn't awful, I'm sure I'll need the help. In high school I had trouble getting through *The Great Gatsby,* and that was written in this century," he explained sheepishly.

"I think I'm up for the challenge," Emily replied shyly.

Just then, a short man wearing a rumpled plaid shirt and wrinkled khaki pants rushed in. His wavy black hair stood on end and his untrimmed beard held remnants of the sugar donut he was finishing as he dug through his worn leather briefcase. After extracting some papers he perched himself on the corner of the long Formica table that served as his desk and said hello.

"Good morning, class. Sorry I was a few minutes late. I was copying off my syllabus," he explained.

Emily groaned inwardly. Just when she thought she had escaped!

"My name is Fisher Lawrence. You can call me Professor Lawrence, but I prefer Fisher. If you bought your books already, you may have noticed there is only one text for this class. Before you get too excited, let me explain that there will be other required reading, but I don't like to choose that without first getting to know those who will be reading it. As the semester progresses and your personalities emerge, I will let you know what I come up with. *Pride and Prejudice* will be a good start, however."

The professor then handed out several sheets that were stapled together, asking those in the front row to please pass them back. When everyone had a copy, he continued.

"You'll notice as you look at my syllabus that I have very few hard and fast rules: I require that you do the reading; I require that you attempt to participate in classroom discussions; and I require you to join me for class on the appointed days if at all possible. Of course, I do understand there will be days when the sun is shining just so and the wind is whispering your name and being inside would be a crime, even for a class as thrilling as mine. On those days, go with my blessing. I trust you not to take advantage of my generosity." He gave a crooked smile. "Beyond that, there are a few papers to write, but nothing a bright group like you can't handle, I'm certain."

Emily flipped through the three-page syllabus. The first page outlined the "rules" he had just gone over; the following two were filled with quotes from great English authors. At the top of each page was a different fish stamp. It took Emily a minute to understand the significance, but then she remembered her teacher's name was Fisher. *Too bad Professor Lawrence wasn't in charge of putting together the syllabus for U.S. History,* Emily thought wryly.

They were excused a few minutes early in exchange for promising to read the first fifty pages of *Pride and Prejudice* by their next class meeting. As John and Emily exited Garfield Hall together they discussed their rather odd English teacher.

"I can't believe he gave us permission to ditch class whenever the weather is good. True, this is Seattle, but the sun still shines every now and then," John said.

"I think that's just his way of letting us know he wants us to *want* to be there," Emily said. "It's so nice to be treated like an adult and trusted to show up. I don't think I'll ever be able to call him by his first name, though."

"I won't have a problem with that. I just hope I can do the work. It's still English," John said, "and I'm sure it'll be hard, no matter what Fisher says. But on to more pleasant subjects. What are your plans for lunch?"

Emily's heart beat a little faster. Things seemed back on track with John, and now he was asking her to lunch!

"Nothing, really," Emily replied, struggling to sound casual. "I have Music Appreciation at two, but I'm free until then."

"Great. Then let's see what culinary delights await us in the cafeteria, shall we?" John said with a flourish, waving his arm and bowing low.

As they headed across the quad, Emily noticed that the beautiful fountain she had sat near at the welcome barbecue was foaming like a rabid dog. John followed her gaze and quickly explained.

"It's dish soap," he said dismissively.

"Dish soap?" Emily repeated.

"Yeah, I heard some guys in my dorm talking about it last night. Someone always does it the first day of classes. You empty a bottle of dish soap in the water and it turns into a bubble bath."

John was still talking about the fountain, telling her how he had heard that on St. Patrick's Day one of the fraternities dyes the water green, when they reached the line to get into the cafeteria. It stretched an entire block, almost reaching the campus post office. They found plenty to talk about, though. They compared schedules and determined they only had English Lit together. Then John told her about the frat party he had been invited to a week from Friday.

"It's one of the more low-key fraternities," he explained. "Dan and I thought we would just stop by to see what Greek life is like. Maybe you and Zoey would like to come?"

Emily wasn't sure. She was afraid it would end up being one of the off-campus parties Nick had described. But John was persistent and promised they could leave if she wasn't having fun.

John noticed her hesitation. "C'mon. Why not go with an open mind? Maybe you'll have a really good time. You might even want to join a sorority when you see how much fun it is," he encouraged.

Just as she was about to decline, Emily remembered that Ryan had practically ordered her to stay away from all frat parties. Here was the perfect opportunity to prove that she could make her own decisions.

"I doubt that I'll want to join, but I'll consider going to the party." After all, it seemed wrong to condemn something without getting the facts firsthand.

After lunch Emily made her way across campus to the building where her Music Appreciation class was held. Apart from chorale or band, Madison High didn't offer much in the way of exposure to music, and Emily was looking forward to expanding her knowledge on the subject. In her eagerness, she arrived nearly twenty minutes early. The classroom was actually a large practice room, with chairs set up in a circle. Emily settled herself with her back to the door so she wouldn't be too close to the teacher and began thumbing through her textbook.

Emily tried to focus on the biography of Mozart she had turned to, but her eyes kept darting around the room. *This place has got to have killer acoustics,* she thought. She had never sung anywhere that looked so professional and couldn't resist playing around a little now. Class didn't start for fifteen minutes, anyway. At first, she sang softly to herself, but soon she got lost in the song, one of her favorites from chorale last year. She was halfway through the chorus when she heard the door creak. Emily's eyes flew open and her cheeks burned as she found an attractive woman in a dark flowing dress staring at her.

"Sorry to interrupt you," the woman said.

"Uh…I was just fooling around," Emily stammered. "I didn't think anyone else would be here this early."

"No problem. I like to arrive a little early myself and collect my thoughts," the woman explained, smiling. "I'm Professor Jamison, by the way."

"Of course," Emily said, remembering they had yet to be introduced. "I'm Emily Stewart."

"You have a beautiful voice, Emily. Have you had much training?"

Now it was Emily's turn to stare. She had always thought it was just her parents who thought she was talented. "Not really. I was in a group in high school and I do a little singing in church, that's all."

"Well, I'm in charge of Tradewinds, a small singing group here on campus that's looking for a few fresh voices. I'd love to have you try out," Professor Jamison invited. "We practice several hours a week and there is traveling involved so you have to have the time to put into it. But anyone who has participated will tell you it's worth it for the trip to the regional competition in Victoria alone."

Emily could hear her parents' challenge—to find a way to use what they saw as her God-given gift—echoing in her mind. What could it hurt to find out a little more?

"When are tryouts?" Emily asked.

"Next week, so there's not much time to decide," Professor Jamison said. She went on to explain the tryout process to Emily after asking about her range and quizzing her on why she thought she might be right for the group.

"I don't mean to give you the third degree, but I don't just look for talent. I want people who really enjoy singing and are a good fit for the group. We spend a lot of time together here and on the road, so it's important that everyone gets along."

Emily thanked her, then turned her attention back to her textbook. It sounded like a big commitment. She would need to give it some real thought. As she read, music suddenly filled the room.

"I like to have a little music playing as my students arrive. It puts everyone in the right frame of mind for the class," Professor Jamison explained when Emily looked up.

Music Appreciation turned out to be even more interesting than Emily had hoped. The students spent an entire hour with their eyes closed and their heads resting on their desks, listening to music. Their assignment was to let their minds create pictures to accompany the sounds that were filling their ears. It was so peaceful.

I wish all my classes could be this easy.

11

mily thought the weekend would never arrive. Her schedule for Friday had seemed light—only French II and Algebra with a free afternoon—but from the minute Madame Moreau said *"bon jour classe,"* Emily knew she was in over her head. It seemed she had forgotten all her French over the summer and there would be no review. Subsequently, her "free" afternoon was spent making French flash cards and conjugating irregular verbs.

Her dad had tried to convince her to sign up for Spanish when she began taking foreign language courses in high school. It was much more practical, he argued. *Practical, schmactical,* Emily had thought. Her head filled with images of smoky cafés and beret-wearing Parisians eating baguettes, Emily signed up for French class. Now, she tried to conjure up those distant romantic images as she quizzed herself, but they wouldn't come.

By the time Zoey knocked on her door at seven o'clock, Emily was all too happy to leave France behind and spend an evening in Seattle. They had decided earlier to get some dinner, then take in a movie at one of the several bargain theaters surrounding the university.

"Nothing with subtitles," Emily warned as she grabbed her coat.

"No problem," Zoey agreed. "After spending all afternoon with my history book, the last thing I want to do is read a movie."

Just as they were walking out the door, Ryan appeared. Emily gave him a quizzical look. It seemed like a lifetime since he had helped her move in.

"I thought I'd stop by and see how you were doing," Ryan said. "Mom and Dad said they hadn't heard from you since we left, and I just wanted to make sure you were okay."

"Of course I'm okay," Emily said, a little huffily. "I called last night to let them know how the first day of classes went, but no one was home. I figured I'd try again in the morning when I know everyone will definitely be there," she explained, amazed that Ryan had the gall to check up on her like she was a baby, especially after their talk last Saturday.

"I was just worried. I remember my first week away from home was rough, and some of the kids in my orientation group are finding it hard to adjust. I wanted to make sure you weren't," Ryan said.

"Kids? Some of the *kids* in your group?" Emily repeated with a raised brow. "May I remind you, you're only one year older than those 'kids'?"

"You know what I mean, Emmie. Uh, sorry, I mean Emily," he said, quickly correcting himself. "Anyway, I was going to ask you if you wanted to come out for coffee with a bunch of us. It's open-mike night at The Cup & Chaucer and a friend of mine is gonna perform a few songs he wrote," Ryan offered, regaining his composure.

"Thanks, but Zoey and I are gonna catch a movie," Emily answered, motioning to her new friend.

As they said their good-byes, Cooper came down the hall.

"Hey, Ryan, what are you doing here?" she asked.

Emily couldn't believe it. Cooper, who rarely spoke to her even though they inhabited the same room, had no problem becoming chummy with her brother in just seven short days. How typical of Emily's life.

"Cooper's in my orientation group," Ryan explained, adding, "I didn't know you guys were roommates."

With that, Ryan seemed to forget his sister as he and Cooper talked animatedly. Emily took the opportunity to make her escape.

Once outside, Emily turned to her friend. "Can you believe him?" she asked.

"He was a little condescending," Zoey admitted, "but it's sweet the way he was concerned. My brother never even speaks to me, let alone checks up on me."

"Consider yourself lucky," Emily said.

"Well, we're rid of him now so let's go eat," Zoey proposed.

Neither girl had a car, so they were limited in how far off-campus they could go. But the main street that bordered the University had several movie theaters that catered to the college crowd, and restaurants were abundant, too.

After checking the starting times at a quaint little movie house, they wandered down Broadway. Zoey thought Café Septiéme looked good, but Emily refused to eat anywhere French after her morning with Madame Moreau. Instead, they decided on a vegetarian restaurant called The Purple Onion. The dim room was lit only by purple stained glass lamps that hung low over the tables. Once they were seated Emily noticed those tables were made from mismatched inlaid tile, each one different from the next.

Their waitress, whose name tag read "Starr," had a nose ring and Crayola-red hair. She also had a very flat stomach which, Emily couldn't help noticing, she showed a lot of with her gauzy blouse tied well above her waist and her crinkled black skirt resting low on her hips. Emily tried to imagine what her parents would do if she came home looking like that. She couldn't.

Zoey led off, ordering the vegetarian burrito while Emily, eager to try something new, opted for the curried pasta salad. Starr had recommended it, assuring her it wasn't too spicy. As their waitress left to put in their order, Emily spotted a large rose tattoo on her back. She began to question the wisdom of allowing someone who had no clue about her taste in food to select an entree for her. Especially when that someone had a tattoo and a ring through her nose.

Emily decided she was wrong to worry as soon as she took her first bite. Her salad was delicious, and she finished every last bite along with several of the chewy whole wheat tortillas the girls had found waiting in a basket on their table. Zoey proclaimed her meal wonderful, too, and the girls christened The Purple Onion their new favorite place before heading down the street to the movie theater.

Dinner wasn't so filling, however, that they didn't have room for snacks at the movie. Armed with chocolate-covered peanuts, Red Vines, and large drinks, the girls settled into their seats. A sappy romantic comedy was just what they were in the mood for, and the movie didn't disappoint.

"That's the way love should be," Zoey said dreamily as they left the theater two hours later.

"When he gave up that job he really wanted in St. Louis to stay with her," Emily said, "it was the perfect romantic gesture. Can you imagine someone doing that for you?"

Zoey admitted she couldn't, but it sure would be nice.

Later that night, while she lay in bed reading *Pride and Prejudice,* Emily found herself relating closely to the main character, Elizabeth Bennett, and her struggle to hold out for love, not just to "make a good match." Emily felt a similar struggle. She really wanted a relationship, but she was holding out for someone she truly loved. As she wondered if Elizabeth would get her happy ending, Emily couldn't help wondering if maybe John Wehmeyer was hers.

Before she had too much time to think about it, Cooper came in, gushing about the coffee house she had gone to with Ryan and his friends. It was just like a place she and her high school friends hung out at back in New York City, she said, and the music was wonderful—a sort of alternative folk sound.

With Cooper's taste in music, her recommendation didn't carry much weight. And Emily couldn't help feeling a little annoyed. *I asked Ryan to give me some space and now he's hanging out with my roommate.*

It was close to midnight, but Emily was too keyed up to sleep. She decided to run a hot bubble bath and soak in it until her mind was completely empty. While the tub was filling, she gathered the thick green candles she and Holly had purchased for their room and set them on the edge of the tub. As she soaked by candlelight she felt every muscle in her body relax until brothers and roommates and French verbs simply disappeared.

When her fingers began to resemble dried apricots, Emily decided it was time to dry off. She wrapped her robe around her and reached for the door knob, but when she pushed, the door was stuck. After struggling with it for a few more minutes, Emily took two steps back, then threw her body against the door. That worked a little too well, sending her flying into the sink area where she came face to face with a big burly guy standing in the middle of the room. All that time in the tub became wasted as Emily felt her muscles tighten back up. She pulled her robe more tightly around her and, with her heart beating in her throat, tried to decide if she should run or scream.

12

efore Emily could make a decision, a tall blonde came out of Kenzie's room, strode up to the intruder, and put her arm around his muscular shoulders.

"Hi, I'm Beth, Kenzie's roommate," she said, as if nothing were wrong. "I see you've already met my boyfriend, Greg." He nodded and smiled, obviously feeling more awkward than Beth.

"I'm Emily," a still shaken Emily managed to get out. Then, recovering a bit, "I thought Kenzie didn't have a roommate. When did you move in?"

"Oh, Greg and I just brought my stuff down tonight. We're both from Tacoma, and since it's less than an hour's drive I've been commuting this week. I only have classes on Tuesdays and Thursdays, anyway. I wasn't planning to live on campus at all—I'd rather stay at home so I can be closer to Greg—but my parents are convinced I won't get the whole college experience unless I do the dorm thing for at least a year, so here I am."

As much as she had been looking forward to going away to school, Emily had a hard time understanding Beth's position. Since she didn't know what to say to her suite-mate's declaration, she just nodded her head. Then, realizing that she was still standing there in her robe, she excused herself.

And she had been worried about Cooper having guys over! Not that it still couldn't happen, but it seemed like a much more immediate possibility with Beth. Emily wondered if Kenzie would say anything to her roommate. Well, at least Emily had been wearing her new robe. At home, she used to wear one of her dad's old T-shirts. That would have been beyond embarrassing.

Emily didn't see Beth the rest of the weekend, so even if she had been in the mood to brave the subject of overnight male guests she couldn't have. Instead, she busied herself by getting a head start on her reading for history and reviewing the algebra lesson from Friday. She also called her parents. It was nice to hear familiar voices, and they assured her they hadn't been concerned at all when they hadn't talked to her during the week.

"We just asked Ryan if he had run into you, that's all," her mom said. She added that they'd been out to dinner on Thursday, explaining why they had missed her call. "We know you are perfectly capable of looking after yourself," Mrs. Stewart continued. "You're a very strong person, Emily, and besides, you are in our prayers every morning so we know you are in good hands."

With a promise to watch her mailbox for the package her mom had sent, Emily hung up the phone. Talking to her family made her realize how much she missed them, but Emily was definitely enjoying her first taste of freedom. It was nice to come and go as she pleased, and she even enjoyed knowing she alone was responsible for getting herself up in the morning and making sure she ate right or finished her homework. If finding strange men in her bathroom at midnight was the price she had to pay for her independence, she could handle that.

Emily didn't see John until Tuesday in English Lit. She tried discussing *Pride and Prejudice* with him before Professor Lawrence arrived, but he admitted he hadn't even made it through the first chapter.

"The names make it impossible to read. There are way too many Miss Bennetts for me to keep straight," he complained.

Emily tried explaining that only the oldest daughter was Miss Bennett. The others were called by their first names or both names when being introduced.

"It's not that hard once you get the characters straight," she told him.

John seemed skeptical, but said he'd give it another try. Emily was glad she was able to convince him. Not just because it was assigned and she didn't want to see him fail or quit the class, but because she really liked the book and wanted to share it with him.

Following class they ate lunch together again, and John's presence made the cafeteria's runny tuna casserole seem not so bad. They both made two trips to the cereal bar, though, and as they left John asked her if she wanted to meet him later that night.

"We can get frozen yogurt and discuss the many Miss Bennetts further if you want," he said, his blue eyes sparkling.

Emily agreed before heading across campus to her music appreciation class.

Professor Jamison was already there when she arrived, and

music filled the room. Emily thought she recognized the classical piece, but wasn't sure from where. As she took her seat, the teacher approached her and asked if she had given any more thought to trying out for Tradewinds.

"I don't want to pressure you, and I've only heard you sing once. But from the way you were enjoying the music in class last week, I just have a feeling you'd be a perfect fit," Professor Jamison explained.

Emily felt honored. She had thought it over and decided that she would at least try out, but she hadn't mentioned it to anyone in case she wasn't chosen for the group. "Well, yes. I think I'd like to give it a shot," she said. Professor Jamison looked pleased.

"I'll look forward to hearing you sing on Thursday then," she said as she returned to the front of the classroom.

Emily was still trying to decide what to sing when she met John that night at The Shack. She had done an interesting rendition of "Amazing Grace" in church a few months back. The music pastor had said it showed off her range nicely, but she wasn't sure if that was what Professor Jamison was looking for.

As John slid into the booth next to her, Emily put Tradewinds out of her mind and concentrated on him. He had read the entire fifty pages of *Pride and Prejudice* that was required and was ready to discuss it.

"Hey, I'm impressed!" Emily told him between bites of her dessert.

They talked long after their frozen yogurt had melted and laughed so much Emily's stomach hurt. John kept trying to understand the book, but he still couldn't keep the characters straight and when he retold the story with everyone all mixed up Emily couldn't help teasing him. He still didn't have it straight by the end of the evening, but The Shack was closing so they gathered up their things.

Instead of turning off and heading to his own dorm when he should have, John walked with Emily all the way back to McNeil Hall. A few blocks before they reached their destination, he gently grabbed her hand. As they continued on with their fingers intertwined, Emily thought to herself, *This is the happiest I've ever been in my whole life.*

When they reached her door John asked her again about the frat party Friday night. After her mom's words of encouragement on Saturday, Emily felt confident she could handle anything. Also, she had met a really nice girl in her algebra class the other day who was in a sorority, and she'd made Greek life sound really fun.

"Zoey and I talked it over at lunch yesterday and decided we'll at least check it out," Emily told him.

The smile John rewarded her with was enough to melt her heart, and she was really glad she had decided to go.

13

The next day Emily's homework continued to pile up, and she found it hard to make time to rehearse for the Tradewinds tryout. Not only that, after inspecting each other's closets and deciding they didn't have anything appropriate to wear to the frat party, Emily had promised Zoey that she would go shopping with her before Friday night.

"I want to try something really different," Emily explained. "All my clothes are so casual. John hasn't even seen me in a skirt."

"And you never know, Nick might be there so I need something that will make me look older," Zoey said.

Emily didn't approve of Zoey's obsession with Nick Carerra, but she didn't want to alienate her friend by coming down too hard on her crush. For the time being, Emily decided to just let it go and hope Zoey met someone else soon.

Thursday morning, Emily felt overwhelmed. She had barely rehearsed for her tryout and still had French and algebra homework to finish before Friday. But as English Lit ended and John asked her if they would be eating together again, she found she couldn't say no.

After lunch, she went to music appreciation full of dread.

While eating, she had decided not to try out for Tradewinds and was going to have to let Professor Jamison know. Thursday afternoon was the only time she could shop with Zoey.

It sounded superficial to pick a shopping expedition over something like Tradewinds, but there was more to it than that. With all the fun she was having with Zoey and John, Emily wasn't sure she wanted to commit a bunch of time to a group neither of them was in. Also, she hadn't had time to properly prepare for the tryout. Still, she felt bad, after the professor had been so encouraging and Emily had been curious to see if she was good enough to be a part of the group. But this was her first "sort-of boyfriend" and her first college party, and those things were important, too, she told herself.

Professor Jamison was very understanding when Emily explained she was too busy to try out after all. Instead of feeling relieved, though, Emily just felt more guilty. She knew her parents would be disappointed in her. But Emily was eighteen, and the decision was hers to make. She would find some other activity to get involved in later, she promised herself, once she adjusted to the homework load and her social life settled down.

After class, she met up with Zoey. "Shopping in Seattle is way more fun than back home," Emily exclaimed after they had looked through several funky boutiques and a few thrift shops.

Finally they ducked into a place called Urban Outfitters. The pounding beat inside reminded Emily of Cooper, but in the large warehouse-like store the music wasn't so annoying. Emily and Zoey had made a pact to try on at least five things in each store, even if they were convinced they would look horrible. So far they hadn't bought anything, but the fashion shows in the dressing rooms had the girls rolling on the floor, laughing. This store had definite possibilities, though, and Zoey and Emily had no trouble finding more than five items to try on.

As they modeled for each other, they found they weren't laughing at the outfits they had put together this time, and several things looked really good. The last thing Emily tried on was the winner, though—a black satiny dress that was fitted on top then flowed perfectly from a high waist and ended a few inches above her knee. It had long sleeves and, the best part, a thin chiffon layer over the skirt that made Emily feel graceful and feminine. Near the cash register they found a dainty necklace with black Austrian crystals, strung ever so delicately. The outfit was perfect, making her feel much older. Still, it would take almost all her cash.

"It's a good thing I saved so much money this summer," Emily told Zoey as her dress and necklace were being rung up. "But I think this will have to be my only clothing purchase until Christmas, or I won't be going to many more movies with you."

"I know what you mean. I'm going to have to get a part-time job in the next few weeks. My parents can't even afford tuition, so I'm definitely on my own when it comes to spending money."

Emily nodded sympathetically. Her parents could barely afford to send her and Ryan to school. If it wasn't for a scholarship fund set up by their church for the staff's kids, Emily would be at community college just like Holly.

Despite her finances, Zoey bought a very pretty fuzzy sweater that had been marked down. The pale color looked really nice on her, and she could wear the top to class or on a date. Finally, exhausted from shopping, the girls were ready for something to eat.

"If we pool what little money we have left, we can afford a small junk-food fix," Emily reasoned.

"I'm game."

Emily spotted a '50s diner called Johnny Rocket's and decided it was the perfect place. She pulled Zoey inside where they collapsed onto the red vinyl seats of the nearest booth. They filled the time waiting for their waiter by checking out the selections on the mini-jukebox that sat on their table. It was stocked with '50s and '60s tunes, and the girls had fun singing along to the ones they recognized. They were digging in their purses for stray change when their waiter finally appeared, decked out in white from his pants up to his fast-food paper hat.

"We'll take an order of chili-cheese fries," Zoey said.

"Can I get you anything to drink with that? Maybe a cherry or vanilla Coke?" their waiter suggested.

The girls looked at each other and added up their change. They had enough money for one drink.

"One vanilla Coke," Zoey finally said.

"And two straws," Emily added.

"The straws are on the table," the waiter pointed out dryly before leaving to place their order.

"I guess he was hoping for a bigger order, huh?" Emily asked.

"Well he better watch it or we'll start deducting money from his already measly tip," Zoey threatened.

"I don't know how my stomach is going to react to chili-cheese fries," Emily said. "I'll probably get sick."

"Not me. I have a stomach of iron," Zoey boasted.

"We'll see about that, my friend."

After devouring the entire greasy platter of chili-soaked fries

Emily was sure they would both be ill. As the girls waddled back to campus they tried to talk about the impending party, but the conversation kept returning to how their stomachs felt.

"I will never eat again," Zoey vowed, as she headed down the hall.

"I bet my new dress won't even fit now," Emily lamented as she entered her own suite.

She turned on some soft music as she lay on the bed, waiting for her food to digest. As the sound filled the room, Emily was suddenly reminded of the Tradewinds tryout she had missed. She hadn't thought of it once the entire afternoon. She had been so anxious to be an adult and make her own decisions, but the situations where there was no right or wrong answer were really hard. *I guess I'll have to trust my instincts.*

Just as Emily had that decided, Zoey burst into her room waving something in her hand. Emily knew how her own stomach still felt; whatever was causing Zoey to jump around so much must be really important. Just watching her was making Emily queasy.

"Have you seen the *newspaper*? Have you *seen* the newspaper?" Zoey shouted, jumping on the bed. "No, of course you haven't. I was with you all afternoon and if you had seen this you would have told me. Right? Of course you would have," Zoey concluded.

"Told you what?" Emily asked, but Zoey just continued to babble.

Finally, Emily grabbed her friend by the shoulders and said in a loud, forceful voice, "Get…a…grip!" enunciating each word carefully.

Zoey sat down on the bed, folded her legs, and took a deep breath.

"That's better. Now can you tell me quietly and calmly what you are so excited about?" Emily asked, still using her Sunday School teacher voice.

Zoey held out to Emily a copy of the *Pacific Rain*, PCU's student newspaper.

"Turn to the classifieds on the back page, then go to the section with the heading 'personals,'" Zoey directed. "The fourth one from the bottom, there," she said pointing to a box with hearts around it. "That's what I'm talking about."

Emily looked at the headline. In bold letters it said "To the fair Miss Stewart."

Emily felt the paper slide from her hands.

14

can't believe it! This is exactly the kind of romantic gesture we were talking about after the movie the other night," Zoey gushed.

The rest of the message read: "I have been meditating on the very great pleasure which a pair of fine eyes in the face of a pretty woman can bestow." Emily immediately recognized it as a quote from *Pride and Prejudice*. The message continued: "Counting the minutes until Friday." There was no name, but the ad was obviously from John. Emily felt like her whole body was tingling. She had never received a card or even a note from a boy before…except maybe in elementary school, when the teacher made each student give a Valentine to every other child in the class.

"Clarissa, my roommate, told me that everyone on campus picks up the paper just to read the personals. It's the most popular section," Zoey informed her.

Emily hadn't even known they existed. She had noticed newspapers littering the campus that afternoon, but she had been so preoccupied with her Tradewinds decision and heaps of homework, she hadn't bothered to pick one up. She was grateful that her friend was a little more curious.

The girls spent the next half-hour reading and rereading the rest of the personals, coming to the joint conclusion that none were as romantic as John's. After telling Emily she was the luckiest girl on campus, Zoey once again returned to her own room.

Emily had a hard time concentrating on her homework that night. Whenever she tried to solve an algebra equation she ended up turning all the x's and y's into chubby little hearts, then she would have to start all over. *This surely isn't what Professor Irving had meant when he said show your work,* she thought, ripping another sheet of paper from her notebook. She still didn't feel all that confident about her math skills when she turned in the assignment the next day, but at least it was done.

Emily decided to forgo lunch that afternoon when she learned the cafeteria was serving meatloaf. She stopped by The Shack to pick up an orange and a chocolate cream cheese muffin before going to check her habitually empty mailbox. As she peered into the tiny metal slot she was surprised to find not only a letter from Holly, but also a slip summoning her to the window to pick up a package. Whatever her mom sent sure had arrived quickly.

As she took her place in line she noticed Kenzie in front of her.

"Hey, looks like someone loves you, too, huh?" Emily said.

"Excuse me?" Kenzie said, turning to see where the voice was coming from.

"You know, the package. I think my mom is afraid I'm not eating, and so she sent me some cookies," Emily volunteered. "Is yours from your parents, too?"

"Maybe. Probably not," Kenzie said, a little guardedly.

Just then the clerk returned with a medium-sized padded envelope and handed it to Kenzie. It had a mailing label on it with a company logo, Emily noticed, so apparently Kenzie was right.

"Hmm. No telling. I think it's just a blouse I ordered." She pulled the envelope tight so Emily couldn't read the address.

Emily didn't want Kenzie to think she was being nosy so she let it drop. Her own package was a big box that her nine-year-old brother Josh had obviously addressed. Her name was written in huge block letters with several colors of felt pen and there were intricate drawings of several different kinds of spacecraft decorating the sides. Josh planned to be the first Stewart on the moon. Eventually he would build a house there so they could all come visit, he promised. Lunar vacations weren't high on Emily's wish list, but she didn't tell her brother that. And seeing his drawings now when she was far from home made her smile.

She and Kenzie walked across the campus together, and Emily felt comfortable enough to open up a little.

"So, I notice you finally have a roommate," she began.

"Sort of. She's gone so much I've started referring to her as 'The Phantom,'" Kenzie replied.

"Well, I was lucky enough to run into her and her boyfriend the other night as I was getting out of the tub," Emily said. "Do you think he'll be around a lot?"

"Like I said, she's not around often, but she did bring up the subject of him staying on the couch every now and then so he didn't have to drive back to Tacoma late at night," Kenzie confided. "I didn't know what to say, so I told her she'd have to talk to you and Cooper, too."

"Oh, great!" Emily wailed. "Push it off on us."

"Well I didn't want to be the bad guy all by myself," Kenzie explained, shrugging her shoulders and smiling.

"How do you know I won't tell Beth I think it's a marvelous idea? We could all sit around together on Saturday mornings and watch cartoons in our pajamas," Emily said with a mischievous look in her eye.

"Assuming he wears pajamas," Kenzie said, tucking her shiny brown hair behind her ear and smiling her dimpled smile.

Emily gave her suite-mate a horrified look before erupting into laughter.

"We'll definitely have to have a talk with Beth," she said.

They were still laughing when they arrived at the dorm, but when they heard yelling coming from their room they became serious and rushed through the door. They followed the noise into the bathroom where Cooper was doing battle with their worn out shower curtain. When they found her, she was perched on the edge of the tub, trying to reattach the mildewy plastic sheet to the rings on the rod above.

"They're ripped," Emily said, pointing to the holes where the rings were supposed to go.

"I know, but I'm trying to tape them," Cooper explained.

"Wouldn't it be easier to just buy a new one?" Emily suggested gently.

"Yes, and I plan to do that tomorrow, but I wanted to take a shower before going out tonight without spraying water all over the floor," Cooper said.

"There must be something we can use for now," Emily said, walking to her bedroom and looking around. A blanket was too heavy; a towel wasn't big enough. Then she spotted a bright box tucked away on a high shelf.

"Hey, Cooper, why do you have a game of Twister?" Emily yelled into the other room.

"What?" Cooper yelled back, before following Kenzie to where her roommate stood.

"You know, right-foot-blue, left-hand-green…Twister," Emily explained, pulling the game down from the shelf.

"Oh, that. It was another going away present. My friend Alex thinks I have a hard time getting to know people, so he thought it might be a nice icebreaker. I brought it with me because it was a gift, but I have no intention of playing it, so don't even ask," Cooper warned.

"I wasn't suggesting we play it, but if I remember correctly, doesn't it come with some kind of plastic mat?" Emily said.

"You're brilliant!" Cooper said excitedly, giving Emily a quick hug. "And I have a hole punch in my drawer. It'll be perfect!"

Emily was a little shocked by her roommate's sudden show of affection. She was usually so matter of fact and didn't seem to care much for Emily. *This date must be a really big deal,* Emily thought.

The next half-hour was spent hanging their new shower curtain. Afterward, standing back to admire their handiwork, the girls decided they liked it so well they would keep it up permanently. It was only when Emily's stomach rumbled that she remembered she hadn't had lunch. She left Cooper to shower and downed her orange and her muffin before plugging in the iron. There were still a few more hours before the party, but she wanted to have everything ready.

Thinking back over the afternoon's events, she was still surprised by Cooper's friendliness. Emily felt wary, but she hoped it signaled a turning point in their relationship. It was probably hard being so far from home and knowing no one. Maybe Cooper really wanted to be close, but like her friend Alex said, she had a difficult time getting to know people. Emily decided to try a little harder in the future.

Two hours later Emily stood at the mirror, almost ready. She sprayed a little perfume on her wrists and used gel to slick her wavy hair back into a sophisticated look, leaving a few wisps down to frame her face. She loved the light sweet-smelling scent because it wasn't too flowery or too fruity. Ever since Holly had given her some for Christmas two years ago, she hadn't worn anything else.

The dress looked even better now that it was pressed, and Emily had applied her make-up carefully, using a smoky shadow to highlight her blue eyes and finishing up with lipstick in a tawny-rose shade. On most days, she just wore blush, mascara, and a little something on her lips; she was always amazed at how different she looked when she took the time to do it all. As she fastened her new necklace, she hoped John would be glad she had taken the time, too. Just then Cooper returned from Kenzie's room where she had gone to borrow some nail polish remover. She stared at Emily.

"Wow, you look really nice," Cooper said.

Emily wished her roommate hadn't sounded so surprised as she offered the compliment, but she was grateful just the same.

"Thanks, Cooper. Zoey and I are going to a party over at one of the frat houses, Pi-something-something. I can never remember," Emily explained.

"Well, that's a great dress. It would look better without the price tag, though," Cooper teased.

As Cooper saved Emily from looking like Minnie Pearl by snipping the tag for her, there was a knock at the door. Knowing that her suite-mates were busy, Kenzie volunteered to answer it. A minute later she popped her head in to let Cooper know her date was in the living room. Emily tried not to laugh as Cooper ran to her bed and started frantically searching for something, throwing articles of clothing in all directions.

"Gee, I'd love to stay and help, but I promised Zoey I'd meet her in her room and I'm already late," Emily said, excusing herself. "But have a great time. I hope he's worth it."

Cooper was so busy pulling on a stretchy gray top and slipping into her shoes at the same time, she barely looked up. But Emily thought she heard a friendly grunt from that side of the room. As she walked through the bathroom, still picturing Cooper struggling to get ready, Emily was surprised to find her brother sitting on the couch.

"What are you doing here?" she started to ask, but before she could finish her question she knew the answer. "You're Cooper's date?" Emily half asked, half stated.

"I promised to take her up in the Space Needle, then we're having dinner," Ryan answered, oblivious to his sister's annoyance. "Where are you going all dressed up? You don't even look like yourself."

"Well, thank you. And you look nice, too," Emily tossed back sarcastically.

"I didn't mean you don't look nice. I'm just so used to seeing you in shorts and no make-up," he explained, sounding a little exasperated. "Now, where did you say you're going?"

"You know very well I didn't say where I was going, but if you really want to know, Zoey and I are meeting some friends from our orientation group at a party," she told him.

"Will the guy from the newspaper be there?" he asked, catching Emily off guard.

"Yes, he will," she answered, refusing to give him any more information. After all, he was the one who showed up in her dorm room uninvited—by her, anyway—and started giving her the third degree.

She reached for the doorknob, but he wasn't done. "I hope you know what you're doing," Ryan said in a tone that clearly implied he thought she didn't. "You just met this guy, after all."

Emily let go of the doorknob and turned back to her brother, determined to put an end to this.

"And you just met Cooper," she pointed out, "so let's get this cleared up. I am going to a party with some friends. I will not be drinking, smoking, or probably even dancing. I am meeting a very nice guy there who seems to think I'm nice, too. We will probably talk and listen to music, then he may walk me home. Most likely before midnight. Can you please tell me what is so wrong with that?"

Ryan looked defeated.

"Look," she continued, softening a bit. "Mom and Dad trust me to make my own decisions. Why don't you?"

"When was the last time they went to a college party? I know what it's like out there and I know what most guys are like. I just don't want you to get hurt," he said.

"I understand that, but I need to learn this stuff for myself. I don't want a bodyguard. Now I'm late and Zoey is waiting. Are we clear on this? I don't want you checking up on me," Emily said, trying to sound firm.

Ryan nodded, but didn't look completely convinced. When she left him he was sitting on the avocado green couch staring at his hands. As Emily walked to Zoey's room she tried to put the image out of her mind.

15

Before Emily could even knock, Zoey was out the door. She looked great in her skirt and new sweater, Emily assured her. Then Emily did a little twirl so Zoey could admire her outfit. As they walked Emily told her friend about Ryan taking Cooper out. Zoey agreed it was weird.

"I don't know what I'd do if my brother ever started dating one of my friends," she admitted. "Not that you and Cooper are friends, exactly."

As they reached Greek Row, the side street that was home to PCU's fraternity and sorority houses, Emily let the subject drop. With the loud music blaring from so many of the windows it was difficult to hear each other anyway. Finally they found the address John had given them, and timidly walked up the steps. Emily was surprised to find that it looked just like any ordinary house except for the big wooden Greek letters stuck on the front and the college students pouring out onto the lawn.

Emily and Zoey stuck close together and made their way into the living room in search of John. Once there, they saw what seemed to Emily like several hundred people although, in reality, it was probably fewer than a hundred. It didn't matter, though, since John wasn't among them.

They didn't have any better luck in the kitchen, but they did run into Zoey's roommate. She had a glass of something in her hand and seemed very excited to see Zoey, even though they had been together in their room only an hour ago. Clarissa gave Zoey a really big hug and told her three times how glad she was they were roommates. Moving into the dining room, she soon disappeared among the couples who were trying to dance amid the wall-to-wall bodies. The girls exchanged puzzled glances before stepping out onto the patio. It felt nice to get some fresh air at least, they agreed.

Once her eyes adjusted to the darkness, Emily spotted someone sitting off to the side in a lawn chair. Upon closer inspection, she saw that it was Dan from their orientation group. Emily was so glad to see someone familiar she almost hugged him. He was puffing on a Marlboro, the tip of his cigarette giving off a weird orange glow in the black night. She hadn't known that Dan smoked, but wasn't too surprised. Smoking seemed to be pretty popular on campus, from what she had gathered during the past week.

"Have you seen John?" Emily asked, trying not to sound too eager. "We were supposed to meet him here."

"We walked over together, but we got separated pretty soon after we arrived," Dan said. "I looked for him for awhile, but couldn't stand all the noise so I ducked out here. I'll help you find him if you want."

The three of them braved the crowds again. Once they were back in the kitchen Emily realized how thirsty she was and looked around for something to drink. Dan noticed her scanning the counters and guessed what she was after.

"There's some kind of rum punch in the fridge and kegs of beer in the upstairs bathroom," he volunteered.

"Isn't there anything nonalcoholic?" she asked.

"Are you kidding? The fraternity throwing the party isn't gonna waste good beer money on something that won't give them a buzz," Dan explained.

Emily felt like she was expected to know that. She wondered if John had known that when he invited her. And if he was so anxious to spend the evening with her, why was he nowhere to be found? But John had promised her that he didn't drink and that the party would be relatively tame. *If this is tame, I'd hate to see wild,* Emily thought.

Just as she was about to give up and go home she saw John across the room. When he finally saw her too, he quickly put down the Styrofoam cup he was holding and made his way over to her.

"Some party, huh? I didn't think I'd ever find you," he said, as he put his arm around her shoulder and leaned down to whisper in her ear. "You look fantastic," he breathed.

The music was loud and Emily could feel the bass rhythm vibrating in her chest, but she had no trouble hearing John's words. She beamed up at him, forgetting the last half hour.

He asked her if she wanted to dance, but they couldn't even get into the dining room past the crowd so they stood in the kitchen instead. John told her about the fraternity brothers he had been talking to and how they wanted him to think about pledging.

"It would mean I could get out of the dorms and at the frat house they have their own cook. Just think about it, Em, no more cafeteria food," he said enthusiastically.

Emily tried to share his excitement, but she liked the dorms. Not only that, if he didn't eat in the cafeteria that meant no more lunches together after English Lit. She hoped her disappointment didn't show.

Dan and Zoey were still there, comparing notes on an art teacher they both had. Emily was about to propose the four of them go somewhere before someone got lost in the crowd. But as she opened her mouth to speak, two upperclassmen approached and cut her off.

"Hey, Johnny, can we get you another brew?" offered a guy wearing a fraternity sweatshirt and baseball hat.

John declined without looking at Emily, then explained, "This is one of the guys I was telling you about."

"Don't believe a word he said. I'm totally innocent of all charges," the guy protested, laughing a little too loudly. A minute later he let out an even louder belch and punched his upperclassman buddy in the arm.

Emily would have been offended that John hadn't introduced her, but she figured that if this was how these guys always acted, they weren't people she wanted to meet. She tried not to judge people without getting to know them first, but Emily had a feeling that in this case, her instincts were right.

Before she could bring up leaving again, the upperclassmen were dragging John off to look at some pool table or something. He gave Emily a helpless look as he was led away, but she noticed he didn't protest too much.

Even without having had anything to drink, Emily had to go to the bathroom, so after making Zoey and Dan promise not to budge, she wandered upstairs. She found what she was looking for quickly enough, but there was a line of people in front of her. Not seeing any alternative, Emily leaned against the wall and settled in for a long wait.

Thirty minutes later, it was finally Emily's turn and she quickly went inside. There were two large metal kegs in the bathtub, but no toilet paper anywhere. She dug around in her purse and finally found a wadded up napkin. It was a little dirty and lint clung to it, but it was better than nothing. As she made her way back down the stairs a few minutes later, Emily was almost knocked down by a girl trying clumsily to make her way to the bathroom. It was too late, though. As soon as the girl passed her, Emily heard a gagging noise and turned just in time to see her throw up all over the stairs and herself.

Having narrowly escaped being a part of that mess, Emily decided she'd had enough. She pushed past the crowds of people to get to the kitchen where she announced to Zoey and Dan that she was leaving. They had found a deck of cards and were killing time with a few hands of gin, but were only too willing to abandon their game and join her. John was nowhere to be seen.

With three of them it was easier to clear a path and they made it to the front door fairly quickly. Once they were outside they gulped fresh air as if they had been underwater for hours. But their relief was short lived. As they crossed the lawn, Zoey spotted something familiar in the bushes. It was the embroidered sweater Clarissa had been wearing earlier. As they looked around for its owner they were amazed to find her sprawled on the neighbor's lawn, bits of mud and grass stuck to her clothes. She looked like she was sleeping, but they when they went to wake her, she wouldn't budge.

16

S he's not asleep, she's unconscious," Dan told Zoey, pointing to a large bump on the girl's forehead that was already turning purplish. Zoey looked very worried about her roommate.

"What happened? Did someone hit her?" Emily questioned worriedly.

"Nah," Dan answered. "Looks like she probably just bumped her head on the sidewalk when she passed out. She's very drunk."

He didn't need to add that last part. They could smell the alcohol clinging to Clarissa's breath and even her clothes, but at least they knew she was breathing. As Zoey paced nervously, Emily sprang into action, helping Dan take control of the situation.

They propped Clarissa up and gently shook her, speaking calmly but firmly. When she didn't respond after several minutes, they decided they would need to get her home. It was going to be a long walk, though, if she didn't wake up.

Emily and Dan each took one arm and looped it around their necks, with Clarissa hanging in between them like an injured player being helped off the field. Injured players usually had one good leg, though, and were at least able to hobble; Clarissa was dead weight as they dragged her down the street. Zoey followed behind with her roommate's sweater and Emily's purse.

"At least her head isn't bleeding," Zoey said, trying to find something positive to say. Dan and Emily just groaned and kept walking.

They were only a few blocks from the university, but it seemed like an eternity before they reached McNeil Hall. Emily couldn't help feeling self-conscious dragging Clarissa across campus, but she was amazed that no one gave them more than a curious glance. Maybe this was more common than she thought.

Once inside Zoey and Clarissa's room, their drunk charge still didn't come around. Emily wracked her brain for some sort of medical rule to apply to the situation. *Starve a cold, feed a fever. Use direct pressure to stop bleeding. Don't move an accident victim.* None of these applied. But then she remembered falling off her bike when she was eight. The next thing she had known, she was sitting on the counter in her bathroom and her mom was applying a cold compress to the bump on her head.

All afternoon, Emily had sat on the couch with a pounding headache, trying to stay awake because the doctor had told Mrs. Stewart it would be dangerous if Emily lapsed back into unconsciousness. Emily also remembered Ryan teasing her, telling her that if she fell asleep she wouldn't wake up and he would get to keep all her toys. Spoiling her brother's fun had been enough motivation to keep her conscious.

Emily wasn't sure if Clarissa's biggest problem was the bump on her head or the alcohol, but the bike crash was the closest situation she had to compare it to, so they propped Clarissa up in a desk chair and Emily wet a washcloth in the sink. When she placed it on Clarissa's forehead, the girl's eyes fluttered open. She tried to say something, but the words were unintelligible.

Emily, Zoey, and Dan cheered triumphantly anyway, not caring that they couldn't understand their patient. At least she was awake, and they weren't going to have to call an ambulance. Emily had been really worried for a while as images from that article on alcohol poisoning flashed through her mind.

With Clarissa becoming more alert, the trio tried to decide what to do next. A cold shower might clear her head, they agreed, but she wasn't really able to stand yet. They were stumped, but then Zoey suggested black coffee. Dan was quick to nix that idea, explaining that it was only a myth that drinking coffee sobered people up. Emily was more concerned with keeping Clarissa awake than getting her sober, so she voted in favor of the caffeine remedy. Dan admitted it would probably help in that area and offered to go get a cup for each of them.

Zoey was feeling antsy and was anxious to be doing something, so she insisted she would get the coffee. Clarissa was her roommate, after all, she said. Dan had done so much already. She grabbed a stack of quarters from Clarissa's desk and was out the door before he could argue with her. Emily returned to her nursing duties, rinsing out the washcloth once more.

Clarissa was a little more coherent now and kept insisting she was fine, although she couldn't focus her eyes on anything and didn't seem to even know who Emily was. She complained loudly that she wanted to lie down on her bed, but as she stood up to make a move in that direction, she landed on the floor in a heap. Dan rushed over and helped her up while Emily grabbed all the pillows she could find to prop her up on the bed. She only agreed to let Clarissa near it if she promised to sit up and try to stay awake.

Once Clarissa was settled, with the washcloth on her forehead and a magazine to look at, Emily collapsed into a desk chair. *This certainly hasn't been the night I imagined,* she thought, looking down at her new dress and picking off a few dirty blades of grass. As she did, she noticed several muddy smudges from where Clarissa had leaned against her. She wondered if she would be able to get them out. When she looked up again she noticed Dan sitting across the room. For a minute, she had forgotten he was there.

"I don't know what we would have done if you hadn't been with us tonight," Emily said. "There's no way we could have made it back to the dorm with her by ourselves."

Dan shrugged it off, seeming embarrassed by the attention. "I've had some experience in this area," he said, but didn't explain further. Emily, having had enough surprises for one evening, was afraid to ask.

"You know, you don't have to hang around if you don't want to. I think we have things pretty much under control," Emily said, but Dan shook his head.

"I think I'll stay if you don't mind the company, at least until Zoey gets back. You never know when Clarissa will decide she wants to try going for a walk, and if that happens I don't think you could get her back to bed," he said.

So they settled in for a long night of keeping watch. Since Clarissa was in no shape to read, looking at the magazine Emily had given her quickly lost its appeal. Adamant that Clarissa not go to sleep, Emily moved next to her on the bed and motioned for Dan to take the desk chair she had just vacated. While Clarissa obviously wasn't up for a major philosophical discussion, Emily thought talking might help pass the time. At first they talked about classes, the horrible cafeteria food, adjusting to their roommates. Whenever Emily asked Clarissa anything, she just moaned, but at least she was awake.

Running out of topics, Emily began to ask Dan about his family. He was reluctant to tell Emily much about himself, but she eventually pried some information out of him. He grew up in San Francisco, was an only child, and had come to PCU to study art. Emily had just begun to tell him about her own family when Zoey returned with the coffee.

Clarissa didn't want to drink anything, but with everyone ganging up on her, she finally relented. She complained with each swallow, though. Emily didn't like coffee either, but since she needed the caffeine, she sipped at hers slowly and pretended it was hot chocolate.

They sat around talking until 4:00 A.M., then decided it was probably safe to let Clarissa get some sleep. She had been really nasty ever since the coffee woke her up a bit, and had spent the last several hours yelling at them for not letting her lie down, or pushing Emily's hand away whenever she tried to replace the washcloth. As she got under the covers still fully clothed, Clarissa glared at them before closing her eyes.

"If she was going to lapse into a coma I think she would have done it by now," Dan assured the girls before he and Emily said good-night to Zoey and made their way sleepily down the hall. At Emily's door she thanked him again for his help as she fished for her keys.

"Like I said, it was no problem. Actually, aside from Clarissa nearly dying, I had a pretty good time," Dan said, stifling a yawn.

"Me, too," Emily was surprised to admit. "I wish John could have joined us, though."

"I'm sure he'll be sorry he missed it," Dan answered, not sounding sure at all. He looked like he wanted to say more, but Emily had her keys in her hand by then. Dan made sure she got inside, then gave a final wave and took off.

After undressing in the dark, Emily slipped silently into bed. It was the first time since they moved in that Cooper was asleep before her. As her head hit the pillow she wondered what Dan had been about to say, but before she could come up with anything, she was out.

17

Emily didn't wake up until almost noon the next day, and even then her head felt all fuzzy. She couldn't begin to imagine what Clarissa's head must feel like.

Good. She deserves it, Emily thought. *What would she have done if we hadn't been there to bring her home? And what happened to the friends she came with?* Emily sure hoped Zoey's roommate had learned her lesson. She hated to admit it, but Ryan had been right about frat parties. Still, she was glad she had gone— if only to prove to herself that she was perfectly capable of handling that kind of situation. She certainly wouldn't be attending any more of those parties, though. She could think of a million better ways to spend her Friday nights.

Emily was working on getting the stains out of her new dress when Cooper came in carrying a small paper bag. She sat on her bed, pulled out a huge bagel, and started spreading some odd-colored cream cheese on it.

"So, pretty late night, huh?" Cooper asked before taking a big bite of bagel.

"Yeah, I hope I didn't wake you," Emily said.

"It's not possible. Once I'm asleep I never hear a thing,"

Cooper said. "Actually, the first few nights here I had trouble falling asleep because it was too quiet. In New York it's noisy twenty-four hours a day. There's traffic and car alarms and sirens all night long and you get really used to them. In fact, their sounds are kind of comforting to me. Sort of a big city lullaby. Here, all I hear when I sleep with my window open is the sound of crickets chirping. It's just creepy," she explained with a shiver.

Emily couldn't help laughing. "I'm sure most people would find the sound of sirens wailing all night much creepier."

Cooper shrugged, licking cream cheese off her finger. They were getting along so well, Emily decided to tell Cooper about the party and keeping vigil all night over Clarissa. Cooper didn't looked shocked at all.

"It was the first time I ever saw anyone drunk," Emily said, feeling really young.

"You're lucky. Once, when I came home late from my friend Claire's, I found a woman passed out in the elevator in our building. She was drunk and had been riding around in there unconscious. I had to get the doorman and he called the paramedics, but by the time they arrived she was awake so they just escorted her to her apartment," Cooper recounted. "It sounds like you handled things fine last night," she added.

"Thanks," Emily said.

"Hey, you haven't had any breakfast, have you?" Cooper asked.

"No," Emily replied, looking down at her robe. "I thought I should get dressed before venturing out of the dorm."

"Well now you don't have to venture out. I have real honest-to-goodness New York bagels with veggie cream cheese. You haven't lived until you've tried them," Cooper told her.

Emily appreciated the gesture, but was a little skeptical. "I'm really more of an English-muffin-with-raspberry-jam kind of person," she explained.

"These will win you over. Here," Cooper said stuffing a bagel half in Emily's hand. "You see, the trick is to get the bagel crunchy on the outside and chewy on the inside. Not many people can do that outside of New York, but I found a little shop across town that seems to have mastered it. These are as close to perfect as I've found away from home."

"I have to admit they are pretty good," Emily said, crunching loudly. "Thanks. I didn't realize how hungry I was."

As she ate, Emily wandered over to Cooper's shelf and peered into the Sea-Monkey tank. "They're coming along nicely," she said, motioning to the spinning microscopic shrimp.

"Thanks," Cooper responded, rolling her eyes. "I'll pass that news on to Claire the next time I e-mail her. She'll be glad to hear it, I'm sure."

"You e-mail messages to your friend? How cool," Emily said. "I'm completely computer illiterate."

"It's really easy. I'll show you sometime." Cooper offered. "If it wasn't for e-mail I'd never hear from Claire and Alex. They both stayed in New York and as far as they're concerned Seattle is Siberia. They're convinced we still get mail delivered here by way of the Pony Express. New Yorkers can be kind of snobby that way. They can't believe anyone would ever want to leave the city."

"Why did you leave, if you don't mind me asking? I mean, you must miss your friends an awful lot and Seattle is really far away."

"That's the point. I wanted to be far away. I always felt a little out of place in New York, so I wanted to see if I fit in any better somewhere else. Seattle was pretty different and I always liked it here when I came to visit my aunt, so I applied to PCU and here I am."

Emily could understand that. Ryan had always been content in their small town and couldn't wait to get back there over the summer, but Emily loved going places. She hadn't had too many opportunities to travel, but she hoped that would change—that coming to Seattle was just the beginning.

"I can't believe you didn't fit in in New York, though, Cooper."

"It's hard to explain. Here I feel like such a New Yorker, yet when I'm there I feel so out of place. Like in high school, everyone was so into the club scene. Every Monday morning all they talked about was the dance clubs they snuck into over the weekend and the drugs they took. Alex, Claire, and I were outcasts because we spent our weekends at the movies or skating in Central Park."

"Skating in Central Park sounds great," Emily said.

"Oh, no," Cooper explained. "Central Park isn't hip at all. You have to hang out in the Village near New York University and go shopping in SoHo on Sunday afternoons to fit in at my high school. But our church is right by Central Park and Alex loves to skate near the boat pond, so we didn't fit in."

Emily tried not to look too shocked. "You go to church?"

"Yeah. A great church on the Upper West Side. It's one of the things I miss the most, after Claire and Alex," Cooper said.

"But you didn't go anywhere last Sunday did you?" Emily began, then caught herself. "I mean, not that it's any of my business. I just didn't think you were a big church-goer."

"I have to admit the early morning services they have here in Seattle are going to be a test of my faith. Back home church starts at 3:00 P.M., which is perfect since I'm never up before eleven on weekends. But all that will be changing tomorrow, because I'm going to church with your brother."

"That's great," Emily said, then added, "that you go to church, I mean. Not that you're going with my brother."

"Uh, right," was all Cooper said, raising one eyebrow.

18

The weekend was cold and rainy, so Emily spent much of it in her dorm room, staying warm and dry. Zoey joined her for most of Saturday afternoon because Clarissa was suffering from a monster hangover, which they could have predicted.

"She didn't even thank me for helping her last night!" Zoey cried. "What an ingrate. We should have just left her there."

"That sounds a little harsh. Maybe she's just embarrassed about the way she acted," Emily suggested.

"Well I won't be doing it again, so I hope she plans on staying sober," Zoey declared.

They passed the time quizzing each other on the last week's notes from U.S. History. Zoey also had the misfortune of having Professor Holden for that class, but met with him on Monday, Wednesday and Friday. When Emily and Zoey were certain their minds couldn't hold another date or fact, they raided the vending machines at the end of the hall and tuned in to the campus radio station, KPCU. It was weird to hear the DJs on the radio and know they were broadcasting from only a few hundred feet away.

On Sunday, Emily went back to Pacific Christian, but this week Kenzie was with her. They had invited Zoey, too, but she said she had plans. Emily's expectations were much lower than they had been the previous Sunday, and this time she was pleasantly surprised. She and Kenzie were greeted warmly at the door, and they had barely sat down before they were approached by a tall woman with long brown hair.

"Hi, I'm Robin, the college pastor's wife," she explained. "I noticed you girls come in, and you look like college students, so I thought I'd come over and invite you to our weekly Bible study."

Emily and Kenzie introduced themselves before getting further details.

"We meet at our house on Friday nights at seven. It's just a block from the church," Robin said, handing each girl an orange flyer. "Here's a map. I hope you girls can come."

Emily and Kenzie walked home together after the service, but then Kenzie had to go to the library to do some research for a paper that was due the next week. Cooper wasn't around either, and no one answered when Emily knocked on Zoey and Clarissa's door, so she went to the cafeteria alone. The rest of the afternoon was spent doing laundry, studying, and writing to Holly. The letter was seven pages long, and Emily's hand was cramped when she finished, but there had been a lot to tell.

When classes began again on Monday, Emily felt like she was settling into a routine with her studying. Even French II wasn't so bad. Madame Moreau seemed to notice all of Emily's hard work, even complimenting her as she returned last week's homework assignment.

"*Tu fais des progrès,* Mademoiselle Stewart. You are making progress."

It was the first positive thing the teacher had ever said to her. Things were going very well until she arrived at English Lit class on Tuesday and saw John.

"What happened to you Friday night?" he started out, before even saying hello.

"What happened to *you*? I got tired of being almost thrown up on and not being able to find anything nonalcoholic to drink so I left," Emily explained, not sure why she felt so defensive.

"You could have at least let me know you were leaving," John pointed out, still sounding frustrated.

"If I had been able to find you in that crowd I would have, but I didn't know where you'd gone," Emily said, relenting a little.

"Well, next time we go to a party I won't let you out of my sight," he promised.

"There won't be a next time for me," Emily told him. "I've been to my one and only frat party, so if you want to spend time with me it will have to be somewhere else."

"Does that mean you won't be visiting me at the fraternity house if they take me?" John asked.

"You mean you still want to try to join that fraternity?" Emily was amazed. "Why would you want to be part of a group like that?"

"Aren't you being a little judgmental? You didn't even give them a chance," John challenged.

Emily hated being called judgmental. It was one of her pet peeves. Mostly because she feared that at times it was true. But it was hard growing up with a pastor for a father. Right and wrong were always so clear. She had a hard time making allowances for people.

She had been wrong about Cooper, though, assuming she wasn't a Christian because of the music she listened to and the fact that she had slept in one Sunday. And Emily had been pretty hard on the congregation at Pacific Christian, too, expecting things from them that she herself didn't always do. Maybe John was right. But before she could talk to him about it any further, Professor Lawrence came hurrying in, leaving a trail of papers behind him.

Emily was glad to forget her own problems and get lost in Elizabeth Bennett's world again, even if it was only for a little while. She had read another fifty pages of *Pride and Prejudice* the night before and was more entranced than ever. Professor Lawrence complimented her on several of her observations regarding the relationship between the Bennett girls and their parents, but gently chided Emily for not calling him Fisher. John didn't join the discussion at all that day.

When class ended, Emily didn't know if she should leave or wait for John. *I doubt we'll be eating together after that heated discussion,* she reasoned, but in the end, she figured that even if he didn't want to join her for lunch, she should let him know she had thought about what he said. She decided to try to keep an open mind regarding the fraternity brothers, but she was still adamant about not attending any more of their parties. When she approached him he looked uncertain, but after hearing what she had to say he gave her a big smile.

"Wonder what's for lunch?" he asked, putting his hand on her shoulder and steering her out the door.

Things were back to normal by the time they left the cafeteria that afternoon, their stomachs full of Lucky Charms. John even walked with Emily to Yesler Hall where her music appreciation class was. As she felt his hand warm in hers, Emily thought, *This is how I wanted things to be Friday night.* He left her at the door and sprinted off to his next class. She could still smell his cologne as she took her seat and tried to guess the composer of the piece playing softly in the background.

That night their orientation group, or "O-group" as Nick called it, met to see how everyone was surviving college life. Zoey spent a full hour agonizing over what to wear, and of course Nick didn't even notice. John, however, was very attentive to Emily. When he asked her if she wanted to grab some ice cream afterward, she had to turn him down, though.

"I'm sorry, but I have a French quiz tomorrow that I really have to study for and an algebra assignment to finish up," Emily explained.

"Can't you study later? We won't be gone long," he pleaded.

"I really can't. I'm just getting up to speed in French so I need all the study time I can get," Emily said, apologetically.

"I don't understand you," John fumed. "First you leave early Friday night then tell me if I want to see you it won't be at the frat house, and now when I try to spend time with you, you blow me off."

Emily looked at him in surprise. "I'm not blowing you off, John. I have studying to do tonight. If you want to get together another night how about on the weekend? I'll have less studying to do then. I really want to spend time with you, I just can't right now," Emily calmly explained.

John didn't seem appeased. "I might have plans this weekend," he said. "I'll have to let you know."

"Okay," Emily said, trying not to look hurt. As she walked back to her dorm in the dark she replayed the scene that had just taken place. She understood that John was disappointed, but he was acting like a spoiled brat. It had been the same way on the bus after the Mariners game. Whenever he didn't get his way, he got mad, but when he let Emily down, like abandoning her at the frat party he had invited her to, it was no big deal. *Is this what having a boyfriend was like? Is John even my boyfriend?* She was almost relieved to crack open her algebra book. At least it held questions she could answer.

19

The next day, Emily was still bothered by the confrontation with John. In fact, after she left Algebra she was so preoccupied that she walked right into Ryan on her way to the cafeteria.

"Hey, I just stopped by your room, but you weren't there. I need to talk to you about something," Ryan said, helping Emily regain her balance.

She eyed him warily, but when he explained he had a favor to ask she relaxed a little.

"My schedule this semester is a bit heavier than I thought and I'm having trouble fitting everything in," he began.

"You could stop hanging around my room so much," Emily suggested helpfully.

"Or you could spend a little *more* time there," Ryan countered.

Emily had no idea what he meant. She had just been joking about his going out with Cooper. Before she could ask what he was talking about, he continued.

"I hear you stayed out all night last Friday. I thought you were just stopping by that party and coming home before midnight," he accused.

"Where would you have heard that from?" she asked.

"Cooper told me she shared her breakfast with you the other morning because you were tired after being out all night," he explained.

"You're pumping my roommate for information about what time I come home?" Emily couldn't believe her ears.

Ryan looked angry, too, as he tried to defend himself. "I wasn't pumping her for information. She mentioned you were tired and I asked why. She explained. It's not like I'm lurking around your dorm spying on you or anything."

"You don't have to lurk! You seem to be getting more than enough information in other ways. And just to set the record straight—not that I owe you any explanation—I was *not* out all night. I came home early when I realized the party was a drunken mess. As we were leaving we found Zoey's roommate passed out on the front lawn. We took her home and I kept Zoey company while she sat up with Clarissa."

"What about the guy you were meeting?" Ryan asked.

"He stayed at the party," Emily admitted.

"Nice guy," Ryan commented sarcastically.

"He is a nice guy, and it's really none of your business."

"Look, I'm sorry," Ryan apologized. "I just worry about you dating some guy no one even knows, who hangs out at frat parties. At home he'd at least have to pass inspection with Mom and Dad."

"He's not 'some guy no one knows.' And what about you? Did you meet Cooper's parents before you took her to dinner Friday night? How do they know you're not Jack the Ripper?" Emily asked.

"They don't, but I didn't take her to a frat party, either," Ryan argued.

Emily raised her hands in surrender. "Fine. You are every parent's dream and I shouldn't be trusted out after dark. Now can we drop the subject?"

Ryan gave an exasperated sigh. "You know I trust you, Em, I just don't trust a lot of the guys on this campus. Look, I'll try to ease up. I don't want to argue any more either. Besides, this wasn't what I wanted to talk to you about."

"Oh, yeah. You said something about a favor, didn't you? You really know how to butter someone up before asking for something," Emily couldn't help saying.

"I know, and like I said, I'm sorry, but I really need your help. I'll owe you one, big time," he said.

"You might as well ask, after all that," Emily said, curious to hear her brother's proposition.

"You know I have that weekly radio show on KPCU, the Wednesday night Christian music hour," Ryan said, looking for some sign of recognition from his sister before continuing.

Emily nodded. She remembered him mentioning it last year. He had even brought a tape of one of the shows when he came home for Spring Break. His music choices weren't the best, but she thought he came across nicely on the air.

"Well I'm having a really hard time fitting it in this year. There's a class I signed up for that's been switched to Wednesday nights and I really need to take it, but the radio station already had the schedule set and won't let me move to another time slot. The station manager's going to find another show to fill my hour, but until he does I'm responsible for the air time. I've got it covered for tonight; I can miss class this once. But do you think you could do it next week? Please? You know more about Christian music than anyone I know. I'm sure you'd be great and someone will be there to walk you through the whole thing. You won't be on your own." Having finished his big pitch, Ryan took a deep breath and waited for his sister's response.

"I don't think I could be on the radio. Even just a campus station. I would be way too nervous," Emily explained.

Ryan's face fell, but he didn't give up that easily. "Em, you'll do fine and I promise you'll barely have to talk. Just keep the music going, that's the important thing. Please? I really need your help."

It wasn't often that Ryan asked Emily for anything. He always liked to handle things himself, so she couldn't help being a little flattered even if he had acted like such a jerk earlier. She decided she'd give it a try, if it was that important to him. Besides, maybe she could use the favor he would owe her to get him to stay out of her personal life.

"Okay, I'll do it," Emily agreed cautiously. Before the words were all the way out of her mouth Ryan grabbed her and gave her a huge hug. Emily wished she felt as excited about her decision. All she felt was a big knot forming in her stomach, and something told her it wouldn't be going away until the radio show was over.

She was still feeling nervous about the show when she walked into her room. Cooper sat on her unmade bed, seemingly oblivious to the mess that surrounded her, studying while the stereo blared. She looked up from her book and said something that Emily could not hear.

"What?" Emily yelled over the noise.

Cooper searched for the remote control, found it somewhere under her blankets, and pointed it in the direction of the music. Once the room was quiet she repeated her question.

"I said, did Ryan find you? He was here looking for you about half an hour ago."

"Yeah, I just talked to him. It seems like you've been talking to him quite a bit, too," Emily said, getting angry all over again that her roommate had blabbed to her brother.

"Well, it's kind of hard to spend a whole evening with someone and not talk, don't you think?" Cooper reasoned.

"I don't have a problem with you talking to Ryan, I just wish you would leave me out of your conversations from now on," Emily replied a little tersely.

"What are you talking about?" Cooper asked, surprised by her roommate's angry tone.

Emily told Cooper about the confrontation she just had with her brother, ending with, "The whole thing wouldn't have taken place if you had just not said anything to Ryan about me."

"Wait just a minute," Cooper said, sounding angry now, herself. "The whole thing wouldn't have happened if your brother wasn't being unreasonable and overprotective."

It was Emily's turn to be surprised. "Then you agree he was being unreasonable? I was sure you'd take his side on this."

"How could I? He's wrong. I innocently mentioned our little breakfast the other morning, telling him how glad I was that you and I were finally getting to know each other. He asked a few questions and I answered them, assuming it was just polite interest on his part."

"Well now you know it wasn't. I'm sorry. I didn't mean to come down so hard on you, but he's driving me crazy and when I thought you were giving him information I got mad at you, too," Emily explained.

"I know I'm not the easiest person to live with," Cooper said, glancing around at the mess around her, "but I would never betray a confidence. If I had known how your brother was acting toward you I never would have said a word. I'm really sorry he upset you."

"It's okay. I'm just glad you're not both in on it," Emily told her roommate.

"I know it's after the fact, but you can rest assured Ryan and I will be having a long talk about this," Cooper assured her. "I can't stop him from being so overprotective, but I can make sure he doesn't involve me."

20

This time when Emily saw copies of the *Pacific Rain* all over campus, she made a point of picking one up. As she scanned the front page headlines, she tried to tell herself she wasn't just interested in the personals. But halfway through a seemingly endless article on the tuition increase she couldn't stand it any longer. She quickly flipped to the back page and began to read.

Most of the messages were cryptic, Emily found, full of inside jokes that only the people they were meant for would get. It was fun trying to figure them out, even if they were unsolvable. Just when Emily was about to give up, she saw it. She sucked in her breath as she read:

"To the fair Miss Stewart: My attentions have been too marked to be mistaken...I am run away with by my feelings."

She couldn't believe he had sent her another note, another quote from their reading. The help she was giving him with *Pride and Prejudice* was paying off in ways she hadn't imagined. Now she felt even worse about their argument Tuesday night. Maybe he wasn't mad because he didn't get his way; maybe he thought her rejection of his invitation to ice cream was her way of rejecting him. She had assured him it wasn't, but she tried to imagine how she would feel in his place. She wished she wasn't so new to this relationship stuff.

When she entered English Lit later that day, John seemed to have forgotten all about the other night. Emily was relieved. They didn't have any time to talk, as Professor Lawrence was on time for once, but as soon as class was over they headed to the cafeteria. It was nice to feel like they had a standing date even if it involved orange plastic trays and food not fit for human consumption.

"Thanks for the message in the paper," Emily said shyly as soon as she and John were seated. He seemed pleased that she had noticed, but tried to brush it off as not a big deal. Emily had hoped that he might ask her out for that weekend. The other night he had said he might have plans, but she was sure that was only because he was upset. Now that everything was okay again, maybe they could go on a real date. Emily was already planning what she would wear when John got up from the table. He gave her shoulder a quick squeeze, said he had to meet someone, then he was gone. Emily just stared after him.

Her hope that he might call her later proved to be just that. When she hadn't heard from him by five o'clock Friday night she walked dejectedly to the cafeteria. Zoey was spending the evening with some girls from her drama class. Their teacher had offered them extra credit if they went to see a local production of *Fiddler on the Roof* and wrote a short review.

"You're more than welcome to tag along," Zoey insisted before leaving, but Emily wanted to wait and see if she would hear from John.

The cafeteria was the most depressing place on Friday

nights. Apparently, no one who had a life ate on campus then. Emily realized this too late as she sat slurping lumpy cream of potato soup and trying to look like she had somewhere to go.

This is the kind of the thing they should tell you at orientation: Avoid the cafeteria on Friday night. Why is it never the useful information that gets passed along? As she placed her tray on the conveyor belt she vowed never to do this again and headed home.

Settling in for a solitary Friday night in the suite, Emily put on her favorite sweats, raided the vending machine at the end of the hall and snuggled up with her quilt on the living room couch. Cooper had set up her TV in there and Emily figured a few hours of mindless channel surfing would help pass the time. She was clicking past several news programs when Kenzie came in.

"Are you going to that Bible Study tonight?" she asked.

Emily had completely forgotten about it. She wasn't sure she was up for meeting a bunch of new people, but as she started to say she thought she'd skip it, she changed her mind. Ever since she'd arrived at school she had been so worried about friends and guys and being alone that she hadn't given God much thought. She went to church each Sunday because she always had, but her heart wasn't in it. Her whole focus while there was on making friends. She couldn't even remember what the sermons had been on either Sunday. Maybe she was sitting home alone tonight because that was the only way God could get her attention. Well it had worked.

In a matter of minutes she had changed into jeans, brushed her hair, and grabbed her Bible. As they walked across campus Emily felt the stress of the past few weeks leave her body. The sun was dipping behind the university, turning the sky a deep red and she felt at peace with herself. It didn't even bother her anymore that John hadn't called, and she found that it was nice to take a break from thinking about him.

When the girls arrived, Robin answered the door and, to their surprise, remembered both their names. They were ushered into the living room where several other students were already settled on couches, chairs, or the floor. On the table was a coffee pot brimming with hot water and a basket filled with tea bags and packets of instant coffee and cocoa. Emily reached for a heavy blue mug and made some raspberry tea before taking a seat next to Kenzie. As the mug warmed her hands someone began playing a guitar and Emily felt like she had come home.

After they had sung several choruses and closed with a rather solemn hymn, Robin's husband Roger began to speak. He was dressed casually in jeans and a navy PCU sweatshirt and could almost have been mistaken for a student. As everyone found I Corinthians in their Bibles he read a passage in chapter ten about everything being permissible, but not beneficial. Emily found herself drawn in by his gentle manner and had no trouble concentrating on what was said.

"Now this verse relates to food and questions that were being raised about what was okay to eat, but I think in many ways it also relates to other areas of our lives," Roger began. "There are hundreds of situations we face as Christians that are not black and white, things that the Bible doesn't forbid but also doesn't condone. And many of these come up in college, the first time you're away from home."

Emily thought of the frat party and wondered again if it had been wrong to go. Growing up, her choices had been so easy.

There were clear rules and she didn't have to make these types of decisions. Now, as much as she had looked forward to being independent, she was having trouble knowing what she should do in certain situations. But if she couldn't always find clear-cut answers, at least it was comforting to know that others were struggling with the same things, too.

Emily found herself really getting involved in the discussion that followed. They talked about what they each personally believed and how those beliefs were colored not just by their understanding of the Bible, but by society.

"Would we be more tolerant of Christians drinking wine if we had been raised in France?" Roger asked. "Certainly, not drinking at all is the easiest way to ensure not getting drunk, but is drinking wrong?"

Emily wasn't certain. Although she knew her parents never drank themselves, did she think all alcohol should be avoided? Since she wasn't of legal drinking age, she hadn't given it much consideration. But when the question of smoking came up, she thought she'd finally found a position she could argue against.

"That's an easy one. Smoking is definitely not okay because it's been proven to be harmful—so you're purposely damaging your body," Emily said.

"Okay, but then do you feel the same way about someone eating a large plate of greasy french fries or polishing off a box of high-fat cookies?" Roger challenged. "Those things can be damaging as well, so why don't we condemn them?"

Before Emily could decide what she thought about that, Roger continued. "Now don't go thinking I'm encouraging smoking. I'm not. I just wanted to show you how sometimes our standards aren't consistent. We know things are wrong without knowing why. What I hope you'll take away from this discussion tonight is a challenge to learn why. Many people will question your beliefs while you're in college and you need to have thought them through. Remember 'all things are permissible, but not all things are beneficial.' Choose the beneficial and you'll be much happier in the long run."

Emily and Kenzie lingered for a while before heading back to campus. It was so nice to be in a real home with the smell of dinner still in the air, and Robin made them feel welcome. As they left, she invited the girls to drop by any time if they ever needed to talk, and Emily felt like she honestly meant it. It felt good to become part of a church that she had chosen on her own and to be accepted for herself, not because she was the pastor's daughter.

The walk back was quiet, and Roger's challenge echoed in Emily's head. She had been doing quite a few things that were permissible, but probably not very beneficial, at least spiritually. She would weigh things more carefully from now on, she vowed.

She didn't see John again until their "O-group" meeting Monday night, and wasn't sure how to act. Had he not wanted to spend time with her over the weekend? If that was the case, why was he so interested during the week and why the romantic message in the paper? She decided it wasn't very "beneficial" to worry about it so she tried to treat him like she would have before the weekend.

As she sat with John on one side and Zoey on the other, the group went through "sensitivity training" that consisted mainly of taking a quiz, then discussing their answers to questions such as "How would you respond if you found out your room-mate was gay?"

Emily had a hard time responding to several of the questions. She knew the answers that were expected, but she also knew that her beliefs weren't always in line with those expectations. She ended up saying she would respect others' opinions and decisions the same way she would expect them to respect hers. But as the discussion began Emily learned that while tolerance was the big buzzword on campus, that tolerance didn't always extend to Christians. She hoped maybe John would jump in, but he didn't. Emily tried to defend her views calmly. Unfortunately, there seemed to be a lot of prejudice against religion of any kind, and it would take more than one night to undo it.

"Come on, I'll walk you girls back to your dorm room," John offered, as soon as the meeting was over. Once they were back at McNeil Hall, he lingered at Emily's door until she invited him in. He followed her into her bedroom where she had gone to deposit her jacket. She turned to find him examining her side of the room with interest, especially the framed pictures of her family she had on her bookshelf.

"I take it this is your family?" John asked, holding out one of the photos.

"Yep." She identified everyone in the picture for him and explained where it had been taken.

After the quick tour they went back out into the living room where he finally explained his absence over the weekend. Apparently Tom and Doug, the frat brothers she had met at the party, had invited him on a backpacking trip at the last minute.

He had left Friday and hadn't returned until late the night before.

Emily couldn't help feeling relief at knowing there was a reason he didn't call. She wasn't thrilled about John continuing to hang out with those guys from the fraternity, but she didn't really feel it was her place to say anything. After recounting the events of his trip, he surprised Emily by asking her out right then for the following weekend. She agreed, and before he left they made tentative plans to go to a seafood restaurant downtown that he'd heard had great views of the water.

"Thanks for walking me home," Emily said at the door, wishing it was the weekend already.

"Any time."

Emily hoped he meant it. Dinner overlooking Elliott Bay sounded very romantic and she had trouble focusing on her reading for U.S. History the rest of the evening.

Cooper came in while Emily was reading the same paragraph for the third time and began talking despite the book in her roommate's lap. Emily glanced up, eager for a diversion at first. She was dying to tell someone all about her upcoming date. But as she opened her mouth, she thought better of it. Even though they had talked about Ryan, she still felt it might be best to not say too much about her life to her roommate.

The realization saddened Emily, but she didn't want to risk having anything repeated to her big brother, even by accident. However, Emily knew she wouldn't be able to talk without eventually saying something about John so she pretended to be engrossed in her reading. The noticeable lack of response soon killed Cooper's attempts at conversation, and the tall brunette headed to the refrigerator in search of bottled water.

21

English Lit was definitely becoming Emily's favorite subject, and it wasn't just because John was in the class. She really enjoyed reading a book, then examining the author's motives: why the plots twisted and turned the way they did; how their own lives colored what they wrote. And Professor Lawrence had a way of making it all so clear.

Sitting in the cafeteria with John after class, Emily finally told him about the radio show she had committed to doing the next afternoon. "I'm already so nervous I just know I'm going to fall apart on the air," Emily confided.

"I'm sure you'll do just fine," he assured her, but didn't seem too interested beyond that.

"So what do you think I should play? Any suggestions?"

"I'm not really all that familiar with Christian artists, so I'm afraid I can't be much help in that area," John confessed. "I'm still kind of new to the whole church scene."

Emily was puzzled. She thought he'd been going to church for at least a year or two. It was weird to realize that after all the time they had spent together in the last few weeks, there were many things she still didn't know about him.

By Wednesday, Emily was a wreck. She was so jumpy she actually looked forward to French class, eager for anything that might help pass the time until that night when she could finally get the dreaded radio show over with. Why had she ever offered to help Ryan? What had she been thinking?

Emily entered the radio station that night loaded down with dozens of CDs and cassettes. Peering nervously into the booth, she saw a large board filled with hundreds of switches and dials, and swallowed hard. Someone was in the middle of doing a show. Emily assumed it must be Mike, the station manager, since that's who Ryan said she would find there when she arrived.

The large glass door was closed and he was talking into a microphone, so Emily waited until he opened the door and introduced himself. He stuck out his hand, but she still had her arms full and didn't know where to set her music. He laughed, then helped her deposit the tapes and CDs onto an empty chair behind the door before beginning to explain the equipment in the sound booth to her.

"Look, you're going to be on your own for most of the hour since I have a class to get to. But it's just college radio, and your first try, so a few seconds of dead air here or there are to be expected," Mike explained.

This didn't comfort Emily any. Her stomach was in knots as she watched Mike expertly run the board, popping in what looked like old 8-track tapes. He explained they were really commercials for local businesses. He paused to set up the next song and talked easily into the big silver microphone.

Mike turned back to her and explained the basics she would

need to know, but Emily just stared at him, unable to clear the confusion from her mind.

"I'll never be able to keep it all straight," she said, alarmed at the panic in her own voice. Finally, Mike left the booth for a minute, returning with a stack of neon Post-It notes and a pen. Only when he began labeling each switch and button for her did Emily allow herself to breathe a little easier. The period of relative calm didn't last long, though.

"Now remember, you've got all your commercials lined up here, stacked in the order you need to play them," Mike explained again on his way out the door. "And if by some remote chance there is some major catastrophe, I left you the assistant manager's phone number on one of those pieces of paper. Now just try to relax and have fun."

Doesn't he realize that's impossible? Emily thought. As soon as the door swung shut and she was alone in the booth, she panicked. It was hard to catch her breath and she felt really light-headed.

Is this what hyperventilating feels like? The only thing that stopped her from passing out cold was the thought that eventually she would have to come to, and fainting would be even more embarrassing than just messing up the radio show.

All too soon the song Mike had left playing ended. Emily leaned closer to the microphone and heard her voice crack as she began to speak. She said the minimum necessary to introduce the first song she had chosen, then sat back nervously as the music filled the booth.

When she made it to the first commercial break she was still pretty panicked, but at least she had begun to believe she would live through the hour. But just then, as the spot for a local bowling alley ended, her elbow connected with the stack of commercial tapes, knocking them all to the floor.

Emily scrambled to pick up the tapes, but as she was on her hands and knees cleaning up the mess, she realized with a start that there was nothing on the air. Jumping to her feet, she hit the button that would start the next song; in the process she kicked one of the tapes across the tiny room and under a chair. Just then she saw someone enter the station. She waited to make sure the music she put on was really playing, took a deep, calming breath, then reached for the glass door with a trembling hand.

A thin guy with round glasses dressed in the PCU "uniform"—flannel shirt, jeans, and hiking boots—asked timidly, "Is Ryan here?"

Emily didn't want to seem unfriendly, but she was sure the song was going to end any second and she didn't want to be standing in the hallway when it did. Also, she still had commercials littering the floor of the booth. She impatiently explained that her brother wasn't doing the show tonight and she was filling in, before turning her back on the intruder. She cued the next song then looked out through the glass and noticed the visitor was still there watching her.

"Is there something else I can help you with?" Emily asked breathlessly, but the guy with the glasses shook his head. Just as she was about to head back into the booth, he spoke.

"I've been sort of helping Ryan these past few weeks, answering the phone or whatever while he does the show. I'd be glad to stick around and give you a hand if you'd like," the guy said. "Not that I think you need a hand or anything," he quickly added.

"You mean you've done this before?" Emily asked, relief washing over her.

"I've helped."

That was all she needed to hear. She grabbed him and dragged him into the booth.

"Watch out where you step," Emily cautioned, "I had a minor accident." Then she stooped to pick up several more commercial tapes.

Without a word, the guy grabbed a clipboard from its nail on the back wall of the booth and began to organize the commercial tapes, stacking them neatly again. After starting another song Emily leaned over to see what he was doing.

"They're supposed to be in order, but I dropped them," she explained.

"That's okay. This is the play list, and it gives the order. See, they're all ready to go now," he said.

Emily sighed in relief. "I don't know what I would have done if you hadn't stopped by."

"By the way, my name is Ethan," he finally said.

Emily flushed with embarrassment. "I can't believe I didn't even introduce myself after you saved my life and everything. I'm Emily."

With things a little more under control they were able to talk a bit during songs. Apparently Ethan was part of Ryan's orientation group and that's how they met. *There seems to be a lot of that going around,* Emily thought, remembering that Cooper was also part of that group. Ethan explained that he liked talking to Ryan so he started hanging around the radio station during the show.

"So will you be taking over permanently or is Ryan just sick or something?" Ethan asked.

"One of his classes was moved to Wednesday night and the station manager won't let him move the show to another time, so he has to give it up. They're looking for a replacement, but he has to cover the time until they find someone. I am definitely not that someone, though."

"Why not? You seem to be doing okay," Ethan said, sounding sincere.

Emily laughed at the absurdity of his statement. "Have you been listening to the same show I have?" she asked.

"Yeah, and it sounds just fine."

Emily eyed him skeptically. "There's still plenty of time for me to mess things up even more," she said, looking at her watch. "Let's just wait and see what you think at the end of the hour."

"Fair enough."

Another song ended and Emily self-consciously approached the mike. She felt silly making small talk to people she couldn't see while someone she had just met sat there listening. After she read one of the typed announcements Mike had left for her, then introduced the next song, she was able to relax a little, though. During the last third of the show, Emily played her real favorites and finally loosened up some, although she wasn't relaxed enough to add extra little bits of information—such as when the albums were released, stories behind any of the songs, and trivia about the artists—like she had practiced the night before.

When the next DJ arrived Emily gathered up her music and followed Ethan out of the station. As they stepped into the night, she felt like the ton of bricks that had been weighing on her chest was finally removed, but she also felt regret. Now that it was over, she was a little sorry. She had never done anything like that, and it had provided a definite adrenaline rush.

"Toward the end there, you were really getting into the rhythm," Ethan said as they stood in front of the station.

"You really think so?"

"Sure. It's too bad you won't be doing it any more because I bet you could get to be really good."

Emily dismissed his compliment with a wave of her hand.

"I was going down for the third time when you showed up. Thanks for your help, Ethan." Emily said. There was something about him that made her feel calm. He seemed so at ease with himself, she couldn't imagine him stumbling around like she had, knocking things over. In fact, the tension in the booth seemed to noticeably decrease as soon as he arrived. Maybe it was because he was so laid-back himself. Whatever the reason, she was grateful he had shown up.

"Oh, it was no problem," he answered.

"I'll tell Ryan you stopped by if I see him," Emily added. Ethan just nodded shyly and went on his way.

22

As Emily was dumping her armload full of music on her bed, there was a knock at the door and Zoey burst in. Her friend had loyally agreed to listen to the show and give an honest opinion, even though she didn't know any of the music Emily would be playing.

"That was the coolest thing I ever heard!" Zoey gushed. "You were wonderful! I can't believe it. My friend, the radio star. And to think I knew you when."

Emily rolled her eyes, embarrassed by her friend's exaggerated praise, but enjoying it, too.

"Let's go celebrate by raiding the vending machine," Zoey said, and the girls headed to the end of the hall in search of cheese popcorn and licorice.

Back in the living room of the suite they ran into Kenzie.

"Hey, did you hear your suite-mate on the radio tonight?" Zoey asked enthusiastically.

"What were you doing on the radio, Emily?"

"She has her own show," Zoey replied before Emily had a chance to.

"Really?" Kenzie said, looking mildly impressed.

"It's not my own show," Emily protested then went on to explain. "I took over my brother's Christian music hour on KPCU tonight, but it was a one-time shot."

"Oh," Kenzie said. "That's too bad." But something about the way she said it made Emily think Kenzie felt it was anything but.

There was an awkward lull in the conversation. Soon, Kenzie returned to her room while Emily and Zoey pigged out.

The day after the radio show, Emily expected John to say something about it during English Lit. After she'd told him over lunch the other day how worried she was, he had promised to listen. But as they sat waiting for Professor Lawrence he made no mention of it. Finally she broke down and asked what he thought. His face went blank.

"Was that last night? I thought it was next week or something. Some guys in my dorm were getting together a game of basketball in the gym and needed another player. I can't believe I missed it."

Emily tried not to look crushed. It had been an accident. Maybe she hadn't been clear about the time. She knew, though, that if John had something important going on she would be there no matter what. She was saved from responding immediately by the perfectly timed appearance of her teacher.

It was nice to focus on the Bennetts and Mr. Darcy and Mr. Wickham for a while, rather than think about her own confusing love life. At least she still had Saturday night to look forward to, and she was happily anticipating going somewhere off campus and finally getting to spend some real time with John.

That's just what they needed to move ahead in their relationship, Emily was convinced.

Lunch was bland as usual, and she spent the time afterward reviewing for a test in music appreciation. John sat next to her holding her hand in his. When he left her at the door to her class thirty minutes later, he reminded her to pick up a newspaper on her way back to the dorm.

Professor Jamison let them leave as soon as the test was completed, and Emily wasted no time hurrying out the door. She grabbed a paper from a stack in the SUB before stopping to check her mail. There was a letter from Holly and, much to Emily's surprise, one from her sister, Kate. She was anxious to open both, but she couldn't stand waiting any longer to check the personals.

She read as she walked, scanning the back page with each step, hoping she didn't run into anyone while her view was obstructed; she was so engrossed, she might not have noticed if she had. At last she found what she was looking for:

"To the fair Miss Stewart, I'm counting the minutes until Saturday night...."

It made her heart race to know that he was looking forward to their first real date as much as she was. The fact that he had taken the trouble to put another message in the paper seemed like a sign that he really cared. But Emily couldn't help wishing he spent less time sending flowery messages and more time being there when she really needed him, like last night during the radio show. Still, he *was* romantic. Other girls would kill for this kind of attention.

She managed to finish Kate's letter, too, before returning to her room. It mostly contained news of the first day of school and how weird it was to be at Madison High without any other Stewarts around. Emily silently wished she could know that feeling at PCU. She knew her wish wasn't likely to come true, though, especially when she opened her door and found Ryan in her living room watching ESPN while he waited for Cooper. He told her that they were going to study together at that coffee house he had taken Cooper to before, The Cup & Chaucer. Emily was about to head into her room to do some studying of her own before meeting Zoey for dinner when Ryan called after her.

"I just want to let you know that Cooper talked to me. I'm sorry again for the other day. I'll try to stay out of your life from now on. Thanks again for filling in for me last night. I had my roommate tape it for me so I can listen to it later, but I've already heard you did great. Looks like you worried for nothing."

"Well, I'm glad to hear it. It wasn't as bad as I thought," Emily answered, before going to her own room.

Cooper was spritzing her hair when Emily entered, but she set the can of hair spray down long enough to tell her roommate there was a message for her on her voice-mail.

"Thanks for talking to Ryan. It seems to have done some good," Emily said before picking up the phone. Cooper just smiled.

Emily still had a hard time with the system and frequently forgot to check for messages or erased them accidentally before she had a chance to listen to them. This message was retrieved without incident, though, and she was surprised to find it was from Mike at KPCU. He wanted her to stop by the station immediately.

148

Her mind began to race. *Did I mess up the commercials after all? Did I break something? Leave some equipment on that should have been turned off? Maybe I wasn't supposed to let Ethan answer the phones. What if an important message got lost and now Mike blames me?* She couldn't stand the suspense so she left for the radio station immediately. Knowing was always better than not knowing, she had learned, even if the news was bad.

As she entered the building she found Mike sitting behind a desk in the large office next to the booth. He was on the phone, but he motioned to an empty chair. Emily lowered herself cautiously into it, taking in the dozens of posters that covered the walls, most of them boasting musicians or bands she'd never heard of. She felt like she had been called into the principal's office, though Mike didn't look like any principal she had ever met. She had been too nervous yesterday to pay much attention to his appearance, but today she wondered how she could have missed it.

He was tall with short black hair that he wore combed back. He also wore thick-rimmed Buddy Holly glasses and clothes from that same era. Today, he had on stiff, dark Levi's with big cuffs and a red and white bowling shirt with the name "Chet" sewn over the pocket. As he hung up the phone, Emily noticed he was wearing a big silver ring with a picture of Elvis on it.

"So how do you feel about last night?" Mike asked, leaning back in his chair.

Emily didn't know how to respond. Was he upset about how the show went? If so, why bother talking to her about it since she wouldn't be doing it again? It didn't make any sense. But he was waiting expectantly. "Uh, I guess I feel okay about it. I mean, there weren't any really long periods of silence or anything," Emily volunteered.

Mike nodded. "I feel pretty okay about it, too, which is why I wanted to offer you a permanent spot on Wednesday nights. I don't care for Christian music myself, but it's good to offer a variety of programming. I listened to your tape this afternoon. You sounded very natural on the air, at least once you loosened up. So what do you say?" Mike concluded.

Emily was stunned. She was sure she had been called in because she had done something wrong, not something right! Now here Mike was offering her her own show. *This is too much,* Emily thought. But then she realized what his offer meant.

"Oh, I don't think I could do it again, let alone every week. I felt like I was going to throw up throughout the entire show last night. The only thing that stopped me was my fear that if I ran to the bathroom the music would stop before I could return and there would be endless minutes of dead air," Emily explained, immediately berating herself for offering such graphic details of her stage fright to this guy she didn't even really know.

Mike didn't seem phased, however. "Well, if that's how you feel I can't force you to do the show, but if you turn it down there won't be a Christian music program at all. And that would be too bad, 'cause we got several calls last night from students saying they were really glad to hear those artists on college radio," Mike slyly explained. "But if you don't want to do it, I'll just program another hour of alternative rock which we already have too much of. That's all any of the other DJs seem to want to play, though," Mike finished, eyeing her expectantly.

Now Emily was really confused. She didn't want to be the

reason there was no Christian music on KPCU, and she had a feeling Mike was counting on that. Still, she wasn't sure she wanted to go through another night like last night. She asked for a day to think about it and left the station, her mind in a fog.

23

Emily ran into Dan on the way back to the dorm. It was funny, but they really hadn't talked since staying up all night together rescuing Clarissa. Emily saw him at "O-group" meetings, of course, but was too preoccupied with John to spend much time with him. As they crossed campus together, though, Dan asked Emily what she was up to and she found herself pouring out to him the whole long story of the radio show. He was a good listener and didn't rush to offer his opinion, which was a nice change.

When she finally did ask Dan what he thought, he turned the question back on her. "What do *you* think, Emily? You're the one who will be doing the show each week. Check out your own feelings," Dan challenged.

After hashing it out a little longer, Dan did eventually offer an opinion of sorts, gently pointing out that, to him, she sounded like she wanted to do it. She was just convincing herself otherwise because she was scared. Emily mulled that over for a few minutes, then laughingly agreed.

"You know, you're right! How do you do that?" she asked, before adding, "After the show was over last night I did feel a little sad. And while I definitely need some practice, music is something I'm really interested in. I was just afraid I might not be good at it, but if I was that bad they wouldn't have asked me to do more shows, right? I'll call Mike as soon as I get back to my room."

By the time they reached McNeil Hall, Dan had promised to make some posters in his graphic art class promoting the show. His next assignment was to design some type of advertisement, so he would get credit for it as well. They could hang them in all the dorms and on the bulletin boards around campus. Emily was so grateful for his help, she made him join her and Zoey for dinner in the PCU cafeteria. "Just give me a minute to call Mike at the station and tell him the news," Emily said.

Standing in line waiting to eat, they noticed that something actually smelled good and people were leaving the cafeteria smiling. When they finally made it inside, they found out it was "steak and shrimp night." None of them had known such a thing existed, but they couldn't have been happier about it. The steak even looked appetizing, they noticed with astonishment, and there was Caesar salad and thick french fries, too. There were even real tablecloths on the tables and cloth napkins. For once they left the cafeteria satisfied, without having gone near the cereal bar.

Later that night, Emily finally had a chance to read Holly's letter. Holly sympathized with Emily when she heard Ryan and Cooper were dating— "You would think that with hundreds of girls on campus he could find one to date that didn't live in your room!" —and was anxious for more details of John. At the end of her correspondence she casually mentioned the new junior high youth pastor her church had just hired. He had graduated from Bible college in the midwest somewhere, had come to Portland to attend seminary, and was twenty-one years old. She didn't give any more details, but Emily knew her friend well enough to read a lot into the little bit of information provided. Holly had a major crush. Emily would have to write back soon and get more details.

On Friday night, Emily went to Bible study with Kenzie again. She had invited John and Zoey to come along, but both had reasons why they couldn't. Still, she had an even better time than the week before and made friends with Robin and Roger's three-year-old daughter, Kylie, who had been asleep when they were there last week. Kylie quickly became attached to Emily and spent the entire evening snuggled on her lap. Emily hadn't realized until that night how few children she had come into contact with since she arrived at college. There were virtually none on campus.

The lesson that night was from 1 Corinthians 3:12, and was about doing things with your life that have eternal value.

"Think of it this way," Roger said. "At the end of each person's life God will light a big bonfire and everything you've ever done will be thrown into the flames. The Bible says the fire will 'test the quality of your work.' If the deeds you have done are solid they'll remain long after the fire goes out, but if your life has centered around temporary things there will be nothing left but ashes. So I have only one question for you tonight: if your life ended tomorrow would you have anything of value to throw on the fire?"

On that heavy note they closed with a prayer, then hung around talking. Robin emerged from the kitchen with several loaves of banana bread, and the students, eager for anything homemade, devoured every last slice in a matter of minutes. Emily was in a peaceful mood as she and Kenzie walked back to campus, pulling the collars of their jackets up around their necks to protect them against the sudden cold.

Saturday dawned warm and sunny, unusual for Seattle. Emily met Zoey for an early morning jog again, but this time they showered and changed clothes before heading to the caf for one of their monster breakfasts. The girls had an agreement that they didn't talk while they ran, but once they were seated in the cafeteria they more than made up for it.

"Zoey, I still have no idea what to wear on my date tonight," Emily complained to her friend. Then, as if just hearing what she had said, she repeated, "My *date* tonight. *My* date tonight. Doesn't that sound so wonderful? It has such a nice ring I think I could just say it over and over," she said with a giggle.

"Well, if you sit here repeating it for too long you won't have anything to wear and you'll miss your date tonight. And 'John's been stood up' doesn't have nearly as nice a ring to it," Zoey chided.

That was all Emily needed to make her concentrate on her food. She wolfed it down almost without pausing to breathe, then dragged her friend back to the dorm for a fashion show. Cooper was still asleep, of course, so they brought the clothes out into the living room and spread them all over the couch. In between outfits, Zoey raced down the hall to her own room to grab a necklace, a belt, or a pair of shoes that she was convinced would be "just perfect."

In the end, Emily chose a long, flowing floral skirt with a pale green sweater that matched the skirt's leaves. Zoey loaned her a silver choker strung with tiny pearls and one larger teardrop-shaped pearl hanging from the center. As Emily stood in front of the TV modeling for her friend, they decided it was the perfect balance between dressy and casual, and pronounced the search over. Then they lugged all the clothes back into Emily's bedroom just as Cooper was beginning to show some signs of life.

The girls spent the rest of the afternoon in the library studying. When they couldn't stand the quiet any longer they went to check their empty mailboxes, then returned to their rooms to get ready—Emily for her big date, and Zoey for an evening out with Clarissa. The latter two weren't exactly friends, but Clarissa did have a car, and spending time with her was more fun than sitting home, Zoey explained.

From the minute John arrived at the door that evening everything was perfect. It was as if he and Emily were finally in sync. There were no miscommunications or misunderstandings, and he even brought her some pale peach roses which he surprised her with at her door.

He opened her car door first, and as he walked around to his side Emily blinked hard several times trying to make sure she was really awake. As John got in the car she smiled sweetly at him. He looked more gorgeous than usual in a pair of crisply pleated navy pants, a white shirt, and a beautiful print tie. He had even worn a jacket, and Emily was glad that she had spent so much time getting ready.

"That's the place," John said when they arrived downtown, pointing out a restaurant that was simply named Cole's. It was right on the water as he promised, and was beautiful inside. There was a lot of polished cherry wood, and the lighting was soft and romantic. A woman played a harp in one corner of the restaurant, and Emily and John were seated to look out on the bay. The sunset was like something from a movie. Emily ate her seafood salad in a state of pure bliss while John polished off a swordfish steak. Emily had never tried swordfish, but it looked delicious, so when he offered her a forkful from across the table she agreed to give it a try.

"Doesn't it just melt on your tongue?" John asked.

It did, Emily agreed, then turned her attention to her own plate. Between bites they compared places they would like to travel, what they would do if they won a million dollars, and —a favorite question of Emily's—what period of time they would most like to live in.

"I would have to choose the 1950s," John said. "Technology was going crazy, TV was still brand new, you could buy a house for what you pay now for a car, and families stayed together. It was like a Disney movie."

It sounded a little boring to Emily, but she tried to hide her disappointment. *We don't have to agree on everything,* Emily silently reminded herself. Still, it gnawed at her. At the mention of families staying together she couldn't help but wonder again about John's father, but decided not to bring it up when things were going so well. There would be plenty of time to talk about it later.

"I would want to live during the 1800s on a farm out on the

prairie somewhere, with acres of land and no cement in sight," Emily confessed.

John raised an eyebrow at her. "Are you sure? I think you've watched too much *Little House on the Prairie*. It was hard work back then. Besides, if you lived in the 1800s we never would have met and my life wouldn't be complete."

Emily was so perfectly happy she was afraid to say anything and ruin the moment. She just smiled as a faint blush crept into her cheeks. After John paid the bill he suggested they walk along the water. Emily wanted the night to go on forever and probably would have agreed to a swim in the ocean's frigid water if it would have prolonged the evening. As they leisurely made their way down the boardwalk, they stopped in several little souvenir shops to look at the tacky back-scratchers, neon coral, and varnished pieces of driftwood.

"Well, it's getting late," John finally said. "I guess we should start heading back to the car." They reluctantly turned back, retracing their steps past the little stores and fish and chips stands. Just before they reached Cole's, John gently grabbed Emily by the arm and pulled her to the wooden railing over-looking the water.

Once she was next to him, John pulled out a small snow globe Emily had been playing with in one of the shops they stopped at.

"I got this for you so you can always remember tonight," he said, looking so deep into her eyes she was sure he saw her soul. Then he leaned in close and whispered, "This has been one of the best nights I've ever had. I'm so glad I met you. I don't ever want to let you go."

What he said was so beautiful, Emily had tears in her eyes

as their lips met for the first time. It was her first real kiss, and like the rest of the evening, it was perfect. They walked back to the car hand in hand with Emily leaning against John's shoulder contentedly. She felt like a kitten and wished she could just curl up next to him forever.

24

In the following weeks, Emily and John settled into a routine. They saw each other Monday nights at "O-group," and Tuesdays and Thursdays both in class and for lunch. On Wednesdays they met at The Shack for frozen yogurt after Emily's radio show, and they went out on Saturday nights. Of course, the messages in the paper continued. It was nice to be part of a couple, and Emily was enjoying her first relationship so much she had to be careful not to gush.

She and Zoey still hung out during the week and on Sunday afternoons, but it wasn't quite the same. Even though Zoey was busy too, with her new job in the campus bookstore, Emily knew her friend felt a little left out. To make up for it, Emily tried hard to find extra time to spend with her. They started jogging more regularly in the mornings before class, and Emily always stopped by to see if Zoey wanted to join her whenever she went to the library to study. She never got as much work done when Zoey came, but the girls had fun playing hide and seek in the stacks in the basement and trying not to get kicked out for laughing too loud.

Zoey was also spending more time with Clarissa. The night

of Emily and John's big date, the two had gone to an eighteen-and-over club downtown that was owned by a member of some band Emily had never heard of. Apparently they were a big deal, though. Zoey informed her they had been on the cover of *Rolling Stone* magazine. Emily still shook her head, sorry to disappoint her friend, but the name didn't ring a bell.

"It was so cool," Zoey enthused, telling Emily all about it the next day. "Three different bands played. There was a huge mosh pit in the front, and the lead singer kept diving off the stage. Clarissa danced some, but I was afraid of getting pushed to the front. I saw people coming out of there with bloody noses, you know," she finished authoritatively.

"Really? And that's cool? Why would you want to get beat up on the dance floor? That doesn't make any sense," Emily replied, hoping she didn't sound too mom-like.

"To tell you the truth, I don't know," Zoey said with a laugh. "But when you're there it doesn't seem so stupid."

Emily was also spending more time with her suite-mates, except Beth, of course, who was never around. In addition to gathering around the TV every night to watch *Wheel of Fortune* together—Kenzie was a whiz at solving the puzzles, while Cooper spent the whole half hour critiquing Vanna's wardrobe —they had begun making late-night runs to the grocery store for studying provisions. Raw chocolate chip cookie dough was their current favorite, although tonight they were heading to Dairy Queen instead. It was an initiation ritual for Cooper.

"Cooper, it's time you were finally introduced to what is unarguably the finest fast food establishment in the free world," Emily had said solemnly. "You've been deprived long enough."

That was all the invitation Cooper had needed, and she had

even volunteered to drive, eager to show off her newly acquired skill behind the wheel. In New York City there had been no need for her to get a driver's license, she explained, but since her arrival on the West Coast she had passed her test and used her savings to buy the little red Honda CRX they were piling into.

"That would be so weird not to know how to drive," Emily said. "Where I live, everyone counts down the days until they turn sixteen. A lot of them even spend their birthdays at the Department of Motor Vehicles, taking the test, not willing to wait one more day for that little plastic card that symbolizes freedom. To think you waited two years!"

"I never even thought about it," Cooper shrugged. "But now I love driving. I don't know if I can ever go back to the subway."

Over burgers and huge orders of fries, the girls compared their experiences of taking the driver's exam, each trying to top the other. They animatedly recounted details of the crazy mistakes they made, found that none of them could parallel park to save their lives, and learned that they all took the test from a cold, unsympathetic DMV employee who made red marks with way too much enthusiasm.

"We each took the exam in a different state, yet it sounds like we all had the same person giving the test," Emily joked.

"At least we all passed. That's what matters," Kenzie observed.

"I have a little confession to make," Cooper said, looking a bit sheepish. "I failed the first time, actually."

Kenzie and Emily looked at one another in mock horror. "That's it. We're walking home!"

"That's not fair!" Cooper wailed. "I have a license now, see?"

162

she said, digging it out of her purse. The girls leaned in to examine the picture. Of course, Cooper looked perfect, as always.

"Well, okay, I'll risk it," Emily relented, smiling at her room-mate.

"I'll remember that one day when you need a ride some-where," Cooper threatened, trying to look indignant.

For the sake of peace between the roommates, they changed the subject to Beth, who Cooper and Emily hadn't seen in weeks.

"Does she really live with you?" they asked Kenzie skeptically.

"I ask myself that sometimes," Kenzie replied. "She is literally never around. But at least the room stays neat that way."

Cooper and Emily looked at each other and burst out laughing.

"At least I keep the mess on my side of the room," Cooper offered. Emily raised an eyebrow. The mess didn't bother her that much anymore, though. She was just glad that she and Cooper were friends.

Emily couldn't have been happier with the way her freshman year was shaping up, even if every now and then John acted jealous, like when he complained about the time Emily spent at the radio station. For the most part, however, things were good.

One day in mid-October, as he was sitting near the fountain with Emily, trying to finish *Pride and Prejudice* in time for the essay exam Professor Lawrence was threatening to give, John brought up their weekend plans. Emily thought he had forgot-ten all about joining the fraternity, but apparently he had just given up talking about it around her.

"Look, I know we talked about going to see *Casablanca* at that little theater downtown, but Tom and Doug and their girl-friends invited us to go with them on a picnic Saturday night to Bainbridge Island. You know, that island Bainbridge dorm is named after? We sailed passed it on that harbor cruise during orientation week. I figure we can rent *Casablanca* anytime, but how often can we do this? Besides, it means a lot to me that they invited us, and if I want to get into the fraternity I'll need them to put in a good word," John said, almost pleading.

Emily had a feeling it had already been decided that they would go; her agreement was merely a formality. The idea of a picnic appealed to her, but she didn't like the idea of hanging out with Tom and Doug. Still, she had been the one who said no more frat parties, and here John was trying to find another way to spend time with his friends and also include Emily. How could she say no?

"What do you want me to bring?" Emily forced herself to cheerfully respond.

Pride and Prejudice was forgotten as they planned their dinner for Saturday night. Emily would go shopping in the afternoon and get everything ready, then they would take a ferry over to the island before dark.

"You won't be sorry," John promised as he kissed her cheek.

Emily hoped he was right.

25

Despite her misgivings, Saturday turned out to be warm, and Emily was happy with the picnic she had packed. John paid for everything on most of their dates, so Emily was glad to have the chance to feed him, for once. She had picked up fresh fruit, thick ham and cheese sandwiches, potato salad, and big cream cheese brownies, all from a little deli she found on Broadway. She also bought several glass bottles of cream soda. Everything was stashed in her tiny refrigerator until it was time to go.

With a little time on her hands before she needed to shower and get ready, Emily decided to take a walk and go check her mail. Maybe there would be a letter from Holly. Emily didn't find any letters when she peeked into the tiny metal box, but she found a package slip, which was even better. As she stood in line she noticed a familiar face ahead of her.

"Not again!" Emily exclaimed as Kenzie turned around. "It seems we're always getting packages on the same day."

"Well, how about that?" Kenzie responded disinterestedly, taking a padded envelope from the mailroom clerk.

Emily noticed it looked just like the last one Kenzie

received, but decided not to comment. *She sure must order a lot of clothes from catalogs, though,* Emily thought. Remembering the new dress she had bought for the frat party, her only clothing purchase that semester, Emily tried to imagine what it would be like to have enough money to buy things whenever she wanted. Emily was so caught up in her thoughts, Kenzie had to nudge her before she noticed she was being handed a package of her own. She was surprised to find out it wasn't from her parents this time, but from Holly. As she ripped it open while she walked, she found it was filled with homemade cookies.

Emily held the box out to Kenzie who took two of the cookies. Cooper pounced on the care package as soon as they entered the suite.

"Homemade cookies," she cried, grabbing several.

After they all had their fill, Emily turned her attention back to getting ready for the picnic. She was still deciding what to wear as she turned off the water in the shower. She didn't want to seem overdressed, and she certainly didn't care about impressing Tom and Doug. In the end, she went with jeans and a warm corduroy shirt with a T-shirt underneath. But it was still a date, so Emily took time to carefully apply her make-up and thoroughly dry her hair before pulling it back with a headband.

From the minute John picked her up, twenty minutes late, the evening was a disaster. Ryan was in the living room waiting for Cooper again— "Why can't that girl ever be ready on time?" Emily mumbled under her breath—and the last thing she needed was for her brother to think she'd been stood up. It had been hard to seem unconcerned, though, as the minutes ticked by. When he finally arrived, John blamed it on Tom and Doug, explaining as he led Emily out to the parking lot that they'd had a last-minute errand to run.

With their food stowed in the rear of Doug's Blazer, John and Emily climbed into the back seat. She tried to keep an open mind, but she wasn't comfortable from the minute they left campus.

Kristen and Leslie, Doug and Tom's dates or girlfriends or whatever they were—Emily had trouble telling—seemed determined to be unfriendly. The first thing they said to her after being introduced was, "Oh, you poor thing. How do you stand living in the dorms?" Emily quickly found out they were sorority sisters and wouldn't be caught dead living on campus.

"What sororities are you rushing?" Kristen asked, assuming everyone must want to be a part of Greek life. When Emily told them she wasn't joining a sorority at all, both girls' eyes got big and they didn't speak for several miles.

Once they were on the ferry, though, Emily felt a little better. She liked the way they drove the car right on board and then were able to get out and wander around up on deck until they reached the other side.

"If I had to commute, this is definitely the way I'd do it," she told John.

"Not me," he replied. "Give me a nice stretch of freeway any day. This waiting would drive me crazy."

Emily couldn't understand how anyone would pick a crowded freeway over this relaxing ride, but she let the subject drop. She didn't want to argue. Besides, soon enough it was time to head back to the car, since they had almost reached the island. They were already making their way down the metal stairs of the big ferry when they realized Leslie wasn't with them. As they all scrambled back up on deck, they spread out to search for her. Tom had just returned from checking the car, and was in the middle of reporting that she wasn't there, when she suddenly appeared.

"I had to go to the bathroom," she said by way of explanation. But Emily had checked the bathroom and didn't think it was possible she would have missed her. It didn't make any sense. Leslie smelled all smoky, too, but not like cigarettes. Emily wondered what she really had been doing.

They made a run for the stairs as they felt the huge boat lurch to a stop. By the time the group reached the Blazer and got inside, the cars ahead of them had already moved on. Several cars behind them were honking and the ferry employees were motioning angrily to them. No one in their car seemed to care, though, so Emily tried not be bothered either.

Once they were on the island they drove for another fifteen minutes to a state park that had fire pits, a beach, and a beautiful view of Mt. Rainier, which stood majestically across the water. Doug and Tom had even thought to bring a portable stereo so they could listen to music while they ate. As they unpacked their coolers, Emily loosened up a bit. Maybe this would be okay after all. She didn't have to become best friends with Kristen and Leslie, but she could still have a good time.

As she was digging in a paper bag in search of the forks she knew the deli had given her, the other two couples began to dance to a slow song that had come on the radio. At first Emily thought it was sort of romantic, but then they started "mashing face" as Zoey would call it, their hands running up and down each others' bodies. Just as Emily found the plastic utensils, John came over to stand next to her.

"You want to dance?"

Emily quickly glanced up at the others again, embarrassed to be witnessing something so...private. She knew there was no way she would ever dance with John like that and she shook her head without meeting his gaze. She heard him sigh loudly, sounding put out, then stomp over to the Blazer to get his jacket.

After what seemed like an eternity, the radio station took a news break and the group's focus was back on food. They spread out blankets from the back of the car and gathered wood for the fire. *I wish I had brought stuff to make S'mores,* Emily thought, as she watched the fire crackle to life. Oh, well, the brownies would have to do. Emily was so busy with the dinner she had "prepared" for John and herself, and entranced by the view, that she didn't really notice what everyone else was eating...or drinking.

It wasn't until she was cleaning up the trash from their meal that she knew something was wrong. John had gone in search of a restroom. As Emily returned from the garbage can, Leslie was laughing so hard she fell backwards off the log she had been sitting on. No one was saying anything funny, but Kristen, Doug, and Tom soon joined in.

It was then that Emily saw the bottle they were passing around. They had been drinking out of plastic cups earlier, and Emily just assumed they had a bottle of Coke or root beer in the Blazer. But now it was obvious they were drinking something quite a bit stronger. They were so drunk they seemed unconcerned that a ranger or policeman might come by and see them. They were having too much fun to care and they had the empty bottles to prove it.

"Hey, Emily hasn't had anything to drink," Kristen said,

grabbing the bottle from Doug and weaving her way around the fire pit.

"Here, we didn't mean to leave you out," she slurred, shoving the bottle in Emily's face.

"No, thanks," Emily told her, pushing the bottle away.

"What's the matter?" Leslie asked from where she sat on Tom's lap. "Afraid to take a little drink?"

"I'm not afraid, I just think it's stupid." Emily explained as if she were talking to a five-year-old.

"Did she just call us stupid?" Tom asked Leslie, nuzzling his face in her hair.

"I'm not sure," Leslie answered, as if the conversation was too much for her to follow.

Just then John returned and Emily breathed a sigh of relief. They could decide what were going to do together. The whole night was a fiasco, but at least they could leave now.

"Should we call a cab or do you know someone else who might be able to come pick us up?" Emily quietly questioned her boyfriend. Instead of offering his own input, though, John stared at her as if she were from another planet.

"Why would we call a cab?" he asked in total puzzlement.

"How about because we can't drive home with people who've been drinking," she replied hotly.

Emily couldn't believe it when John rolled his eyes at her. "I am not going to look like some kind of baby and cause a big scene. Why do you have to be so judgmental? Why can't you just roll with it? This means a lot to me," he almost hissed.

"Well, my life means a lot to me, and I'm not getting in that car," Emily hissed back.

"We're not leaving yet. They'll sober up in a little while."

"Well, they won't be sober enough."

"Is there some sort of problem?" Doug managed to ask in a somewhat serious voice before he began laughing hysterically.

"I just thought you might like John or me to drive us home," Emily suggested. She wanted desperately to salvage the evening.

"No one else is driving my Blazer," Doug said.

"That's fine, everything's fine," John said soothingly, as if speaking the words would make them true. Even though his so-called friends were acting like complete idiots, he still seemed to care what they thought. Well Emily didn't.

"Everything is *not* fine," Emily almost screamed.

"Now Emily, why not relax a little and have some fun? You're in college now. Mommy and Daddy don't have to find out," Tom said much too loudly, as he draped his arm over her shoulder.

Emily quickly stepped out of his reach and he nearly toppled over.

"What's wrong, Johnny, is your little girlfriend too good for us?" Doug asked. "She didn't seem to have a problem when you were pounding back a few brews with us at the frat party. Don't you like the harder stuff, honey?"

Emily didn't want to believe him. "I thought you told me you didn't drink," she said to John. She waited for him to deny Doug's charge, but her boyfriend wouldn't even look her in the eye. Suddenly, the image of him holding a Styrofoam cup at the frat party popped into her head. If she hadn't been able to find anything non-alcoholic to drink, how had he? Obviously he hadn't. Why hadn't she realized it then?

"Guess that means she doesn't know about the fake ID then, huh Johnny?" Tom blurted out before saying "Oops" and covering his mouth. The rest of the group just laughed.

John didn't even try to deny it, and Emily knew there could be no explanation she would understand. John had probably even been with them when they bought whatever they were drinking now. There was no doubt in her mind why they had been late.

Now Emily began to panic. She was determined not to get in a car with people who were drunk, but it would take hours to walk to the ferry station and it was pitch black outside. She knew she didn't have nearly enough money for a cab. Maybe if she could make it to the pay phone she had noticed at the front entrance of the campground she could call someone back at school. Kenzie had a car and so did Cooper. Clarissa was a possibility, too, although a remote one. With a plan, Emily began to feel a little better and strode over to the campfire to gather up her things.

Kristen and Leslie just laughed and said, "Maybe it's good you plan to stay in the dorms after all. You're not really sorority material." Then Tom rose and whispered something to Leslie about heading down the beach for a little private party, just the two of them. Leslie gave him a long kiss then followed him out toward the water, her hands in his back pockets.

Emily would have been shocked, but she felt too numb for any emotions to register. She hadn't expected much of the others, but how could she have been so wrong about John? As she headed into the darkness by herself, she wasn't really surprised that John didn't follow.

She was only a few feet away when she heard Doug say, "Don't sweat it, Johnny Boy, you're better off without her." She wondered if John believed him.

It was a lonely walk to the campground entrance and Emily

had plenty of time to beat herself up for allowing John to get her into this situation; for allowing *Emily* to get her into this situation. After her talk to Ryan about making her own decisions and deserving to be treated like an adult, she had proven him right. She wasn't as mature as she thought. She wasn't mature at all.

As she walked, she carried on a one-sided conversation with God. *Boy, I really blew it this time didn't I? I was so anxious to have a boyfriend I was willing to do just about anything, and now look at me. I'm stumbling along in the dark. I've been doing that a lot lately, though, haven't I? Stumbling along in my walk with you, ignoring the hand you've been holding out to me, insisting I can make it on my own.*

Well, I can't make it on my own, Lord, and I'm sorry it took this to make me realize it. I tried being in control of my life and now it's one big mess. I know I don't deserve a second chance, God, but if you could see your way clear to giving me one I won't let you down. Please, I really need your help. Not just here on this dark road, but every day. I know now I can't make it on my own.

26

It took almost an hour to get to a phone, with Emily praying the whole way. It was so dark, she had to walk extremely slowly so she didn't trip in one of the hidden holes. *All I need now is to sprain my ankle,* she thought.

When she finally had the receiver in her hand, she tried to decide who to call first. Emily finally chose Clarissa, figuring she would ask the fewest questions, but no one answered. *She must still be out,* Emily said to herself. Next she tried Kenzie, but had no luck. Cooper wasn't home, either. When Emily placed the receiver back in its cradle she had to fight back tears. There was no one left to call but Ryan, and what if he wasn't home?

With trembling fingers, she dialed the university's main line one more time and asked the operator for Ryan Stewart's room. With each ring her heart sank further. Not sure what else to do, Emily placed each call again. Someone would eventually have to get home and the dialing would at least keep her occupied. *Please God, let someone answer,* she whispered.

Finally, after her fourth call to her own room someone answered, but it wasn't Cooper. She couldn't believe it when she heard her brother's voice, but she was so relieved to have finally reached a real live person that she almost didn't care. Almost.

"Ryan, it's Emily. Look, I need a ride home. Can you grab a pencil and write this down? I'm on Bainbridge Island at Fay Bainbridge State Park," Emily explained, reading the name of the park off a lighted sign. "I'm in a phone booth at the entrance and I promise to explain everything when you get here if you'll just come get me now."

"What are you talking about? Where's your date? Why can't he bring you home?" Ryan continued firing questions until he heard his sister sniffling on the other end of the line. She had held it together until then, but relief at not having to walk all night in the dark finally registered.

"I'm on my way, Emmie," Ryan said, his voice filled with concern. After the night she'd had, hearing her old familiar nickname was sort of comforting.

It took another forty-five minutes before Ryan arrived. Emily was never so glad to see anyone in her whole life. She jumped in the cab of his old familiar truck and gave her brother a big hug before settling back against the seat and waiting for the onslaught of questions. She had occupied herself during her long wait by preparing herself for the "I-told-you-sos" she knew were coming. The thing was, Emily felt so bad that there was nothing Ryan could say to make her feel worse.

"Okay, now, start from the top and don't leave anything out," Ryan commanded as they headed for the ferry terminal.

Emily took a deep breath, then told her brother the whole story—from how sweet John had been to her the past few weeks to finding out that a fraternity was more important to him than she was. She really thought she could trust him, but there was no way he might have misunderstood her views on drinking and thought she would go along with a party like the one they had tonight. She could only assume he thought Doug and Tom would be a little more discreet and that Emily might not notice. That way, he could score points with his frat buddies and hang on to Emily, too. When that hadn't worked, he had made his choice painfully clear.

"Go ahead and say I told you so. I deserve it," Emily offered. At least Ryan hadn't brought Cooper along on this little rescue mission. That would have just made it all the more humiliating.

They were aboard the ferry now and Ryan asked if she wanted to go up on deck. She knew there was no way she could possibly enjoy the night view of Seattle or the chilly ocean breeze without thinking of John. And thoughts of him would simply get her angry all over again, so she begged Ryan to stay in the truck.

"That's fine with me. We can do whatever you want. And don't worry. I have no intention of saying 'I told you so.' You had no way of knowing what was going to happen tonight. John seemed like a nice guy and every other time you went out he treated you respectfully. So you weren't thrilled about his friends. I've double dated with some people I'd rather not know myself," Ryan said, smiling at his sister.

He was being so nice, it almost made it worse.

"You did everything right tonight, Emily," he assured her. "All those times I told you that you weren't mature enough to handle these types of situations, I was wrong. If this had happened to me last year I would have probably been too much of a wimp to stand up to those guys. I would have put myself in danger by riding home with them, even though I knew they were too drunk to be behind the wheel. But you didn't do that."

"I can't believe you would have stayed at a party like that, Ryan," Emily said incredulously. "You would never have even been at a party like that in the first place."

"That's where you're wrong. I *have* been at parties like that. That's how I knew what to tell you to stay away from. At the beginning of last year, I hung out with guys like the ones you were with tonight. It was so great to be away from home and able to do whatever I wanted, I went out every weekend. I spent so much time hanging out, in fact, that by the middle of first semester I was failing two classes and doing almost as bad in the other three."

Emily couldn't believe what she was hearing. Her perfect brother had messed up? "So what did you do?"

"I finally woke up. I hired a tutor, did any make-up work or extra-credit my teachers would give me, and studied every spare minute. My semester grades weren't great, but they were passable and Mom and Dad blamed it on adjusting to college. It wasn't a fun lesson to learn, though. If I came down on you a little hard this year, it's just because I was trying to save you from making the same mistakes I did."

"And I appreciate it," Emily assured him quietly, "even if it doesn't always seem like it. It's like I told you before, though. I need to find these things out for myself. There is nothing you could have told me that would have made me see what a jerk John was. I needed to discover that on my own, and now I have."

They were driving through the streets of Seattle by this time, and before Emily knew what he was doing, Ryan had pulled into a 7-Eleven parking lot and had gotten out of the truck. In a few minutes he returned with two large cherry Slurpees. Emily smiled as she remembered how they used to beg their mom to stop for them when they were younger, but she rarely would. "They're just pure sugar," she would tell them disapprovingly. As a result of their earlier deprivation, the older Stewart kids now had them whenever they got the chance.

Emily had no problem polishing hers off. It was the Stewart curse. Most people lost their appetite when they got nervous or upset, but Emily just ate more. Even when she got the flu she could still eat. It was a good thing she went running as often as she did.

By the time Ryan pulled up in front of McNeil Hall, Emily was feeling a tiny bit better, although maybe it was just the sugar. It would take her a long time to get over her disappointment about John, but at least she wouldn't be spending the night in a dark, deserted parking lot.

"Thanks again, Ryan. I don't know what I would have done if you hadn't been around tonight," Emily said.

"No problem. But you would have been fine even if I hadn't come for you. You've never really needed my help. That's why I was so surprised by what you said the day we drove to college. You're the one who is always good at everything. You have a beautiful voice, you make friends so easily, you take over my radio show for one week and they beg you to do it permanently. You know, Mike never once called me in to tell me I was doing a good job. He just left notes on the board pointing out mistakes I made," Ryan said, grinning.

"I'm sure that will happen to me soon enough," Emily protested, but Ryan continued.

"And most importantly, you eased right into college life without making any of the stupid mistakes I did."

"What do you call tonight?" Emily asked in surprise.

"That was nothing compared to my freshman year."

"Well, my first semester grades aren't out yet," Emily said ruefully, thinking of all the hours she'd spent dreaming about John when she should have been studying. "Besides, there's still Kate," Emily consoled Ryan, remembering their obnoxious younger sister. "I think she's gonna need a lot of help when she gets to college, so you might want to stick close by."

"Oh, I'm sure our little Katie would love that," he laughed. "No, I bet you she'll go to school as far away as she can get just to make sure she doesn't have any older brothers or sisters hanging around keeping an eye on her."

"She will if she knows what's good for her," Emily teased, punching Ryan in the arm. She hopped down from the truck and walked slowly to her room, giving her brother one last wave.

When she entered the suite she immediately ran into Kenzie.

"Hey, did you bring one of those for me?" she asked.

Emily had to look down at her hands to remember she was still holding her empty Slurpee cup. "Sorry," she shrugged. "I drank the whole thing."

"Well, I'm always up for some cookie dough, so let me know if you get another craving later," Kenzie said.

"It's a date," Emily agreed, then winced at her own word choice. It looked like late-night runs to the grocery store with her suite-mates would be the only dates she would be going on for a while.

Emily felt a little self-conscious as she stepped into her room. She wasn't sure what Ryan had told Cooper when he rushed out earlier. And even with her brother's assurances that she wasn't to blame, Emily still felt stupid for allowing herself to be so taken in by John.

Her worrying proved to be for nothing, though, for if her roommate had any idea what had gone on that night she didn't show it. In fact, Cooper was stretched out on her bed with a stack of fashion magazines, ripping something out of *Allure* when Emily walked in.

"What do you think of this haircut?" Cooper asked, holding out a picture of a model with short, wispy hair.

"I think it makes her look like a boy," Emily answered honestly.

"Oh," Cooper replied, reexamining the photo before tossing it on the floor. Emily noticed she had already amassed quite a pile of discarded styles.

"You're not thinking of cutting your hair are you?" Emily asked.

"I've had some variation of this same style for several years and now I'm finally free to cut it," Cooper explained.

"What do you mean 'free to cut it'?" Emily queried. "Did your parents want you to keep it long?"

"Oh, no, nothing like that," Cooper laughed. Then vaguely explained, "It was for work."

Emily still didn't understand, but decided to let it go after offering one last opinion. "Whatever reason your job had for wanting you not to cut your hair, I think they were right. It looks great the way it is."

Cooper thanked her for the compliment, but Emily noticed she didn't stop tearing out pictures. When Emily glanced over as another style was thrown onto the ground, her roommate smiled sheepishly.

"Well maybe just a little change," Cooper explained, moving on to a copy of *Harper's Bazaar*.

Emily fell asleep to the sound of paper tearing and spent the night starring in several horrible nightmares. In the most vivid one, she was lost in some very dark woods and Kristen and Leslie were chasing her with a huge pair of scissors, trying to cut her hair.

27

Emily didn't see Zoey until late Sunday afternoon. They had made plans to study together for their big U.S. History exam the following week. If there had been any way she could have gotten out of it Emily would have, but she couldn't lie to her friend and she knew she had no honest excuse. They hadn't been studying for more than five minutes before Zoey casually asked how the picnic had gone. They didn't get much work done after that.

"That jerk!" Zoey screeched. "Just wait until we see him at 'O-group' tomorrow night. I'll give him a piece of my mind— you can count on it."

Emily groaned. "I hadn't even thought about having to see him tomorrow night. I was trying to prepare myself for sitting through English Lit with him on Tuesday. 'O-group' totally slipped my mind."

"He's the one who will need to be prepared when he runs into me," Zoey growled.

"Please don't, Zoey," Emily begged. The last thing she wanted was a big scene in front of all the members of Group 16. She knew that eventually she would have to say something to John, but she didn't plan on saying it with a crowd around.

"Okay, if that's the way you want it. But if you change your mind let me know and I'm all over him," Zoey promised.

Emily assured her friend that she appreciated the offer and tried to change the subject. Thankfully, Emily didn't run into John in the cafeteria, and she and Zoey returned to the dorm without incident. They parted in the hallway because they both had more studying to do, and knew they wouldn't get anything done if they stayed in the same room.

As much as Emily wished she could stop time, she couldn't, and Monday night eventually rolled around. She would gladly have subjected herself to another of Professor Holden's history tests if it would have saved her from seeing John, but she had to go. At least she had Zoey to walk in with. Much to her relief, John wasn't there yet. She and Zoey sat on the couch next to Dan, feeling there was safety in numbers. Emily tried hard to look unconcerned while Zoey tried on Dan's sunglasses, teasing him about wearing them when it was almost dark outside.

Emily was tense through the entire hour-long meeting, even though John didn't show. If he had come, at least she could have gotten it over with. This way, she had to be on guard all night in case he arrived late. The stress took its toll. When she got back to her room Emily curled up on her bed and fell fast asleep, not waking until her alarm went off at 7:30 Tuesday morning.

The next day she made it through her history test okay. Making her way to English Lit, however, was like walking to the electric chair. She took as long as possible to climb the stairs, but finally entered Professor Lawrence's classroom. She didn't know whether to breathe a sigh of relief or to cry when she saw that John hadn't arrived yet. She knew she couldn't endure another hour of waiting like she had last night. Then suddenly she knew she wouldn't have to. John walked into the room and took a seat a few rows over without even looking in Emily's direction.

Fortunately, they had their mid-term that day so Emily wouldn't have to suffer through a long discussion. She could finish her essay test and leave. And chances were, she wouldn't have to run into John on her way out of the classroom, either. As the tests were passed out, Emily busied herself getting a blue-book—a blank booklet students purchased for exams—and pens out of her backpack. The essay question was an easy one. They were to compare and contrast the real goodness of Mr. Darcy with the supposed goodness of Mr. Wickham, and discuss how people weren't always what they appeared to be. Emily remembered how Elizabeth Bennett had hated Mr. Darcy at first and couldn't help liking Mr. Wickham, but how things had changed by the end of the book.

As Emily wrote furiously, glad to have something to keep her busy at last, she couldn't help noticing how much John was like Wickham. He was charming, knew all the right things to say, and was good at covering up what he didn't want others to know of his personality. She needed someone more like Mr. Darcy, she decided, as she ended her final paragraph and rose to turn in her paper.

On her way out the door, John got up and walked to the front of the class, all the while acting like he didn't even see her.

She felt her stomach tighten, but held her head high and walked toward the cafeteria.

After a lonely lunch Emily had Music Appreciation, but when she arrived, she found that class was canceled for the day. There was a note taped to the door explaining that Professor Jamison was sick. Several students from her class whooped or jumped up and down when they read the note, but Emily couldn't muster any enthusiasm. It did give her some extra time to study for her algebra mid-term, though.

And Emily did try to study. But then the snow globe John had bought for her would catch her eye, or she would see the leaf she still had from the scavenger hunt they had won. She knew she wouldn't be able to get any more done until she had some closure. Everything was just left hanging, and she wanted to get to a point where she didn't live in fear of running into John. It was just too hard.

Emily looked at her watch. John should just be getting out of class now. Maybe she could catch him if she hurried. Emily raced across campus rehearsing what she wanted to say, but she was so out of breath when she finally found him she almost couldn't speak. He looked surprised to see her, but pleased, too, leading her to a nearby bench to rest before allowing her to say whatever it was she had come to say.

"Look, John, I don't like the way things ended between us and I just couldn't leave it that way," Emily began.

"I'm glad to hear you say that," John said in response. "I didn't like the way things went the other night, either. You overreacted a little, but I knew once you had some time to think about it you would come around. I mean, I wasn't even drinking Saturday, but it's okay, I forgive you."

Emily had thought she was beyond being shocked, but this was too much.

"*You* forgive *me?* Let me tell you something Mr. Wehmeyer, I didn't come here looking for forgiveness. If I had it to do over, I would act the same way I did the other night, so I haven't 'come around' like you seem to think. I just don't want to have to turn around and go the other way every time I see you on campus. I had hoped you wouldn't want to, either."

"You're the one who turned and walked away from me the other night," John said angrily. "If you want to come back now, just say the word."

Emily sighed. "I'm not saying I think we should keep dating, John. That's over. You lied to me, and you put me in a dangerous position to impress some guys who, from everything I've seen, aren't worth impressing. I can get over that, but I can't stay with someone who would treat me that way. We obviously want very different things from college, and I just didn't see that before," Emily said, relieved to finally have said what was on her mind.

"Well, I'm so glad you found out in time and were saved the trauma of having to associate with me any longer," John retorted sarcastically.

Emily looked at him sadly. "That's not what I'm saying at all. I don't agree with all of the choices you're making, but they're your choices to make. I'm glad we met. I just wish it had turned out differently, that's all."

And she meant it. She couldn't help thinking back to the kiss they had shared next to the water less than a month ago. How had everything changed so fast?

Emily was amazed at the hurtfulness of what John said next.

"It could have turned out differently if you just weren't so uptight, Emily. Go ahead and leave, but don't think I'll be alone long. Kristen and Leslie have lots of friends they can't wait to introduce me to."

The gleam in his eye made Emily shudder. There was no way they were going to be able to resolve things if he felt this way. She turned to go, but not before adding, "I hope they make you happy, John."

28

With algebraic equations coming out her ears, Emily took a break from studying to get some music together for the next day's radio show. She was actually feeling kind of excited about it.

Ethan had become a regular fixture in the studio on Wednesday nights, and she looked forward to his company and calming presence. With John out of the picture, Emily was grateful to have activities to occupy her time. She made a list of all the music she wanted to play and the length of each song, allowing spaces for commercials in between. She then cued each tape to the right starting point and stacked her CDs. With that done, she put in a load of laundry, then zoned out in front of the TV while waiting for the wash cycle to finish.

Every week, Emily was a little more sure of herself in the booth, and the show the next night went smoothly. She was still convinced she had done the right thing by agreeing to do it, but with her heart feeling like it had been run over by an eighteen-wheeler it was hard to listen to songs about love. She tried not to focus on the lyrics, but every now and then a tear would escape as a song took on new meaning for her. She would quickly wipe the tears away, though, before Ethan noticed.

This week Ethan had brought a few CDs of his own, and Emily spent the time between songs looking them over, every now and then asking him a question or two about them.

"Some of the songs are a little obscure, but I thought you might give them a listen and see if any of them are right for the show," he said.

They hung out in companionable silence, and Emily noticed she never felt like she had to entertain Ethan or make small talk. He just did his own thing. When the show was over, he helped her gather up her things and said he'd see her next week. She was still waving to him when Dan appeared.

"Hey, I was going to call you!" Emily smiled up at him. "Thank you so much for the posters. I saw them all over campus today and they look great. You're really talented," she enthused. "But you know, you didn't have to hang them up all by yourself. I would have helped you."

He just shrugged off her compliment. "I had some free time before lunch. It was no trouble."

"Well, thanks just the same," Emily said.

"Actually, I need to talk to you about something if you have a few minutes. Want to go grab a fruit shake at The Shack?" Dan asked.

Emily was caught off guard. What could he have to talk to her about? She figured she might as well find out, so, intrigued, she followed him into the little restaurant and ordered a strawberry-orange-banana concoction from the girl behind the counter.

When they were settled in a creaky vinyl booth, Dan began.

"I need to apologize to you for something. I heard about your break-up with John and I feel really bad."

"Why do *you* feel bad? It didn't have anything to do with you," Emily said, struggling to understand his meaning.

"That's the problem. Since it didn't have to do with me, I told myself I should just stay out of it. It was none of my business. But now I think I might have been able to spare you some hurt," Dan said, a pained expression distorting his features.

"How could you have done that?" Emily asked, genuinely interested.

Dan seemed to be searching for the right words. "There are things I knew about John that I should have told you, but I figured you wouldn't want to hear them. I didn't want to upset you so I kept my mouth shut, but if I had been a real friend I would have spoken up."

"What things?" Emily asked.

"Well, for starters, I knew that although he told you he wasn't drinking, he had a fake ID and was going out with those frat guys on the weekends. He showed it to me the first week of school, before you two really started dating. He was trying to impress me or something, but I told him I wasn't into that. Also, I know he didn't get home from that party until the next morning because after I left you and Zoey and Clarissa, I ran into him and he was just coming in. He wasn't exactly sober, either."

Emily just sighed. She'd known John had lied to her, but this made it all seem so calculated. What had been the point?

"If that's what he wanted to do, why did he ask me out in the first place? There are plenty of girls on campus who would have no problem with his partying. Why not pick one of them?" Emily wondered.

"Not to stick up for him or anything, but I really do think he cared about you. He just has some problems he needs to work out. Do you know how I found out you two broke up? He came into my room last night and was ranting and raving about how unfairly you were treating him. He kept talking about how everybody leaves him. That's a big thing with him."

"What does he mean 'everybody leaves him'?" Emily asked.

"Well, you know his dad walked out when he was real young," Dan began.

"No, I didn't know that," Emily almost whispered. "I could never get him to tell me anything about his father."

"Apparently his family is pretty screwed up. His mom works all the time, his stepdad doesn't talk to him, but he screams a lot, and John's little brother has already run away from home twice. The first time he managed to get all the way to their dad's in Nevada, but their father just sent him right back. He doesn't even want to see them."

Emily felt sick to her stomach. She couldn't imagine not having a good relationship with her family. And she had complained so much about Ryan to John. Now she understood why he was so fascinated by her family pictures that day in her room.

"I bet that's why this fraternity thing means so much to him. He'll finally have a family," Emily reasoned.

"Makes sense to me," Dan agreed. "I just hope you aren't too upset I didn't tell you what I knew earlier."

"Not at all! You did the right thing. I needed to find out for myself. And you were right, I wouldn't have wanted to hear it," Emily said.

"The thing I don't understand is that he mentioned church a couple of times, even though I don't think he was going. It was like he thought he could lie and cheat during the week then show up one Sunday and make it all okay. Like he believed that Monday through Saturday didn't count," Dan confided, looking to Emily for an explanation.

"Well, unfortunately, a lot of people live that way. I was always taught, though, that it all counted. You went to church on Sunday to learn how to live the rest of the week," Emily said.

"That makes a lot more sense. Maybe you're the one I should be going to church with," Dan said.

"I go to a great Bible study on Friday night with one of my suite-mates. You could meet us in front of our dorm at about 6:30 and check it out for yourself," she proposed.

"I'll be there," he answered.

29

Emily dreaded English Lit a little less by the time she reached the room on Thursday. John was already seated and, remembering her conversation with Dan, she forced herself to smile politely in his direction. There was no response in return. At least Emily knew she had made an effort to work things out and because of that she could look him in the eye. It was little consolation, though. Soon Professor Lawrence arrived with their graded tests and Emily was able to focus on something else.

Class seemed to drag on forever, but eventually Emily was free and on her way to meet Zoey for lunch. Emily thought she was doing rather well, all things considered, but her friend had insisted they eat together so Emily didn't just sit there moping around.

"The food is depressing enough without you crying in it!" Zoey had said.

When Emily entered the caf and saw Zoey waving furiously, she was glad she had agreed to come. They laughed all through lunch and Emily was in good spirits as she headed to Music Appreciation. The door was open this time when she arrived, and music wafted out from the classroom.

"Good afternoon, Emily," the teacher said, looking up from her stacks of papers. "I was hoping you'd be here, because I have something to talk to you about."

Emily approached her desk, hoping it didn't have to do with the test they had taken last week. She'd had a hard time keeping all the different composers straight.

"What is it?" Emily asked.

"You remember Tradewinds, don't you?"

How could Emily have forgotten? It seemed like ages since she had contemplated trying out.

"Of course," Emily answered.

"Well, we've had to drop one of our new members from the group, so we're holding another mini-audition with just a few people I've selected. I was hoping maybe you would change your mind and decide to try out after all," the teacher said.

"Actually, it looks like I'll be having a lot more free time than I thought, so yes, I'd love to try out for Tradewinds," Emily informed her professor.

She was still thinking about the audition when she entered her dorm room an hour later. *Now if I could just fill every other waking moment I wouldn't have any time to think about John,* she thought as she kicked the door shut. She stopped short when she saw a beautiful vase full of pale roses on the table in the living room and leaned over to smell them. She inhaled deeply then held her breath, eyes closed, wanting to hold the sweet smell inside forever. Eventually she had to breathe, though, and as she reluctantly opened her eyes she noticed a card nestled among the flowers with her name on it.

She couldn't believe it! She had never had flowers delivered to her before. She opened the envelope with trembling fingers and found that all it said inside was a generic "Thinking of you." She checked the envelope again to make sure it wasn't some sort of mistake, but her first and last name were clearly printed on the front.

"Cooper? Kenzie? Is anybody here?" Emily yelled into the suite. Maybe they could help her solve the mystery. There was a muffled reply from her own room so she headed in that direction.

"Cooper?" Emily yelled again, wondering if maybe she had imagined the first response. The room was obviously empty. But just then someone emerged from under the bed. It looked a little like Cooper, but she was so covered in dust and balls of fuzz that Emily had to take another look. She stared at her skeptically.

"It is so extremely gross under that bed! I am going to have to stop throwing things under there."

It was Cooper all right.

"Sorry to interrupt your little party with the dust bunnies, but did you happen to notice the flowers in the living room?" Emily asked.

"Of course I did. They're gorgeous! Who ever sent those is a definite keeper," Cooper told Emily, as she stood in front of the mirror examining her clothes for stray lint. Then she seemed to think better of her pronouncement and added, "They're not from John are they?"

Emily had eventually told her roommate all about the break-up when she realized that Ryan hadn't said anything. He really was trying to stay out of her personal life and it was nice to know she could talk freely to Cooper and not have to worry about her conversations being repeated.

"I can't imagine they would be. He won't even look at me, and I think I made it pretty clear to him that there is no chance of us getting back together. He did bring me roses once before, though," Emily said, remembering the flowers from their first real date. She had dried them upside down, determined to save them forever, and hung them above her bed with a green ribbon around their stems. Forever unexpectedly ended last Sunday, though, when Emily ceremoniously flushed them, petal by petal, down the toilet. The stems went in the laundry room trash can. She was staring at the bare wall where they had hung when Cooper spoke again.

"John doesn't seem like the anonymous type, though. If the goal is to try to get you to change your mind about the break-up, he wouldn't have sent them with an unsigned card. He would want to get credit for the gesture."

"You're right. I don't think it was John. But who else do I know who would do something like this for me?" Emily asked, furrowing her brow.

"What about your parents or maybe even your brother? They knew you were upset about the break-up," Cooper suggested.

Emily had just talked to her mom last night, feeling a sudden need to tell her how much she appreciated her after her conversation with Dan and his revelations about John's unhappy home situation. Emily had told her mom about the break-up, and she had been very sympathetic. But Emily knew she wasn't the answer to the mystery. And Ryan—well, that was laughable!

"You don't know my parents," Emily explained. "They are

very practical and would never do something so extravagant. A card maybe or a nice long letter, but never a huge vase of roses. And while Ryan and I are getting along, he's not the flower type either. But you ought to know that better than I do. Has he ever brought you flowers?" Emily asked.

"Come to think of it, no he hasn't. He bought me a tire gauge last week, though, so I can properly inflate my tires," Cooper admitted, laughing. "He is a bit on the practical side, now that you mention it."

They were still puzzled when Kenzie poked her head in, looking for some company.

"How many guys have you been alone with in the last week?" Kenzie asked, quickly getting into the mystery.

Emily started to protest, saying she hadn't been alone with any guy since she broke up with John, but then she really thought about it. She had talked to Dan after the radio show, and she and Ethan had spent several hours alone in the booth together. There was even the hour she spent with Mike the other day getting some more training at the station. Technically, she had been alone with all of them. She ran down the list while Cooper and Kenzie listened attentively, but was quick to add that she was sure none of them would have sent her flowers.

"I doubt it was Ethan," Kenzie agreed. She'd known Ethan, a fellow Nashvillian, ever since he'd traveled out to PCU with her and her family at the beginning of the year. "He's more the brother type—at least to me. But then again, he *is* awfully shy when he's face to face with girls. Hmm...."

After much deliberation, the girls finally decided it was most likely some unknown secret admirer in one of Emily's classes.

Kenzie and Cooper made Emily promise to keep her eyes open the next few days for anyone who was suspiciously nice to her.

30

mily spent much of Friday studying people. *Could he be the one?* she thought, as she looked from face to face in her classes, in the cafeteria, near her mailbox. Finally, she decided she had to stop thinking about it or it would drive her crazy. She was glad, when she finally left for Bible study with Dan and Kenzie, to be going off campus where every guy she saw wasn't the potential mystery man.

Afterward, Dan was shooting questions at Emily and Kenzie, and they decided to grab a cup of coffee so they could continue talking.

"Let's try that place Cooper talks about, The Cup & Chaucer," Kenzie suggested.

A few minutes later, they stepped inside the little coffee-house-bookstore. It was like another world. The walls were lined with dark wood shelves that were filled with books. Cozy, mismatched couches and chairs were scattered around the room, and there was a tiny stage in one corner. In another corner a few computers were set up on a high round table with bar stools around it.

As their eyes adjusted, Emily spotted Cooper coming toward them.

"Hey, what are you guys doing here?" she asked, then dragged them off to a spot near the back where Ryan and Ethan were already drinking large cappuccinos. As the newcomers sank down into the overstuffed furniture, Emily introduced Dan. After awhile, a girl appeared at their table to take their order.

"Hi, my name's Maddie. What can I get for you tonight?" she asked.

Emily glanced up at their waitress, who was busy brushing her wild red hair from her face so she could better see her order pad. She was wearing black pants and a white blouse like the other waitresses, but her top was short and revealing, her pants tight. As she raised her pen in anticipation of an order, her armful of silver bracelets jangled melodically.

"I'll have a hot chocolate," Emily decided, pulling her gaze back to the menu. The others quickly chimed in with their orders, too.

The group sat chatting amiably, soaking up the ambiance until their drinks arrived. As they sipped their coffee, or in Emily's case, hot chocolate, they each chose a book from the wall to look at. Emily was delighted when she found a copy of another Jane Austen book, this one titled *Emma*. She was reading a passage from it out loud when a shadow fell across the page. She looked up to see who was blocking her light and was surprised to see Mike from the radio station. He smiled and glanced at the cover of the book before turning his attention to Ryan.

"Thanks for sending your sister over to us," he said. "She's catching on quick."

He and Ryan talked for a few more minutes, then Mike left to join some of his friends at a table near the front. Emily's group lingered for a long time, exploring the books and enjoying each other's company. As they walked home Emily felt contented. She had only thought about John a few hundred times that night, which was an improvement.

In the morning, Emily went running with Zoey, then they stopped at the cafeteria for their traditional huge breakfast. Emily had the rest of the day free so she decided to kill some time by going to check for mail. She didn't really expect to find anything since Holly hadn't even received her latest letter, but, to her surprise, there was something in her box.

She looked at the small white envelope and tried to figure out why it looked so strange to her. Then she realized it was because it hadn't been mailed. There was no postmark or stamp, and there wasn't even a return address. *It must be from someone on campus,* Emily thought. *But who?*

Ripping the envelope open, she found a single sheet of white paper inside. On it was printed: "Look inside the copy of *Emma.*" She examined the front of the envelope again for clues and noticed the writing seemed to match that on the card that came with her flowers. But "the copy of *Emma*"? It must be referring to the book she had scanned at the coffee house.

Once back in her room she compared the note with the card. Emily was sure they were from the same person. She felt strange going to The Cup & Chaucer, like she might be on a wild goose chase. But she was dying to see what she might find in the book. She compromised by deciding not to tell anyone. If no one knew, she wouldn't feel quite so dumb. That decided, she grabbed a light jacket and set out.

As she walked, she wondered again who it might be. Obviously, it was someone who was at the coffee house last night and had seen her with the book. Mike had been there just as she was reading, but she couldn't believe he was the one, although he had been really nice the other day at the station. And Ethan was there last night, too. Dan was even sitting next to her, but didn't he just think of her as a friend?

She was no closer to solving the mystery when she entered The Cup & Chaucer. As her eyes adjusted to the low light she looked at the spot where she had been sitting last night. The deep blue velvet couch was empty, she noticed with relief, and she headed over to it. Scanning the shelf for the novel, she began to worry that the book might be gone. What if someone moved it or found the surprise in the book that was meant for her? Her eyes darted frantically from title to title. Then she sucked in her breath as she saw the red, leather-bound volume.

With the book in her hands she sat on the couch and looked around the room. There weren't many people there, and no one seemed to notice her although she was amazed everyone within a ten mile radius didn't hear her heart pounding. When she couldn't stand the suspense any longer, Emily gently opened the front cover. She found nothing. She turned another page, then another, and still saw nothing but the printed words of Jane Austen. Maybe it was a joke. Cooper, Kenzie, and Zoey all knew about the flowers. What if they were teasing her? But, no, none of them would do anything so cruel.

Feeling desperate, Emily held the book open by the covers and flipped it upside down, shaking the pages. Several tiny dried flowers fell out, followed by a thin sheet of paper. She set each brightly colored flower on the coffee table in front of her then unfolded the note.

"You're too pretty to be sad. Hope the flowers make you smile again. P.S. I like your taste in books."

As she folded the note back up and tucked the dried flowers inside, Emily was no closer to knowing who her mystery friend was. But that didn't stop a smile from spreading across her face.

She placed the book back on the shelf and walked out into the sunlight. As she headed down Broadway clutching the note, she marveled at the idea that someone liked her just the way she was. After trying so hard to be what John wanted and finding that in the end she couldn't, this new realization was a relief.

As she walked, she took out one of the flowers and held it up to the sun. She watched in wonder as the delicate petals were transformed by the light. As she witnessed the flower come to life, she felt a warmth creep through her, too. The last two months weren't anything like she had planned, but she wouldn't change them even if she could. She had great friends, a bunch of new opportunities, and maybe even another chance at love.

As all the possibilities tumbled around in her head, Emily quickened her pace, anxious to get back to campus. After all, her life was finally getting really good. And she didn't want to miss a single minute of it.

NUMBER 2
HOMEWARD HEART

By Lissa Halls Johnson
ISBN 0-88070-948-0

Maddy MacDonald's first year at PCU brings yet another new beginning for the girl who spent her childhood moving from town to town. This time, however, quirky Maddy has made up her mind to set down roots. Unfortunately, that's easier said than done after she finds herself in all kinds of trouble—trouble that threatens her future at PCU.

As it turns out, Maddy's fun-loving boyfriend, Kick, may love fun just a little too much—and he seems determined to get Maddy to join him in his adventures. Yet, even as Maddy strives to avoid the party scene, her mere association with Kick may provide exactly the ammunition a disgruntled coworker needs to get her booted out of the library—and the school—for good.

Will an unfortunate misunderstanding lead to her dismissal from the college? Or will Maddy finally find an anchor for her *Homeward Heart?*

Available at your local Christian bookstore.
If it is not in stock, ask them to special order it for you!

NUMBER 3
TRUE IDENTITY

By Bernie Sheahan
ISBN 0-88070-949-9

Kenzie Dawson, the Nashville-born-and-bred daughter of a Christian record company president, is using PCU as an escape from the pressures that come with being in the Christian music industry's inner circle. How long can she keep up the charade?

Kenzie finds that her reluctance to share the details of her Nashville life with her new PCU friends soon gets in the way. But it takes a budding romance with the musically talented Chris Gallagher, a Seattle concert appearance of longtime family friend and Christian pop star Billy Weber, and an ongoing tense relationship with Emily Stewart—her "Christian music freak" suitemate—to force Kenzie to make some difficult choices regarding the kind of person she wants to be.

Will she finally embrace her background, her Nashville life, and her own remarkable musical gifts? Or will she continue to hide the truth from her new friends, in hopes of creating a new image for herself, apart from her Nashville associations? Meet the real Kenzie Dawson in *True Identity*.

N U M **4** B E R
SPRING BREAK

By Wendy Lee Nentwig
ISBN 0-88070-950-2

Cooper Ellis's life is just beginning to come together. Looking for something different, the ex-professional model has left her home in New York City for college in the beautiful Pacific Northwest.

At school in Seattle she gets a great roommate and snags the guy of her dreams, a starting guard on PCU's basketball team. But after six perfect months together, her boyfriend starts having doubts about their relationship and Cooper's spring break plans are turned upside-down. And it doesn't help matters that just when her relationship is on the rocks, everyone around her seems to be pairing up.

Forced to spend spring break far from her PCU friends, Cooper has a lot of time to rethink her relationships, her decision to attend PCU, and her place in the great, big world. But as she struggles with those questions, God shows Cooper that in order to see his plan she didn't need to go all the way to Seattle…she just had to open her eyes.

Available after September 1996 at your local Christian bookstore.
If it is not in stock, ask them to special order it for you!